A Funny
Old Life

PATRICIA HAYES

A Funny Old Life

TERESA JENNINGS
with PATRICIA HAYES

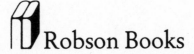

Robson Books

First published in Great Britain in 1990 by
ROBSON BOOKS LTD, BOLSOVER HOUSE,
5–6 CLIPSTONE STREET, LONDON W1P 7EB

Copyright © 1990 Teresa Jennings

British Library Cataloguing in Publication Data

Hayes, Patricia
  Patricia Hayes: a funny old life.
  1. Acting – Biographies
  I. Title   II. Jennings, Teresa
  792.028092

  ISBN 0 86051 692 X

Photoset in North Wales by
Derek Doyle & Associates, Mold, Clwyd.
Printed and bound in Great Britain by
Butler & Tanner Ltd, Frome and London

Contents

Foreword by Patricia Hayes

This book, written with such love and dedication by my daughter Teresa, gives me an excellent excuse for not having written – or ever wished to write – my own life story. Frankly, to do so would have bored me! I have always been much too interested and excited about what may happen in the future to want to dwell on the past. I like to live intensely in the present, mindful of the past, with an eye on the future. Her book has also reminded me of lots of joys that I did not truly appreciate at the time – and of how many agonies I endured over things not worth agonizing over.

I am exceptionally lucky in that I find I get happier and happier as I get older and older. I have been so fortunate in my family, my friends, my acquaintances and my fans. These last always telling me what a marvellous person I am, in spite of the fact that I am definitely not!

My three children know me best, and I am grateful for the fact that they still love me in spite of all my failings.

My character was formed by my Catholic faith, and the love of my life was my father.

Patricia Hayes

Introduction

February 23rd 1988. A day that shall be emblazoned in the memory of actress Patricia Hayes. A day of immense pride for her family, friends and admirers. On that day, Patricia Hayes went to Buckingham Palace to receive from Her Majesty, Queen Elizabeth, the Queen of England, the OBE for her Services to the British Theatre. No one could have been more proud than my mother – except perhaps those of her family who were privileged enough to be with her on that auspicious day.

When the great day dawned, we did not have to look out of the window to know that the sun was shining. It was squeezing through the cracks between the curtains and the window frames and flooding over the wistaria-covered balcony outside my mother's bedroom. Hurray! The thought of splashing about the courtyard of Buckingham Palace in the rain, dashing from archway to archway trying to protect our special hairdos was not an appealing one.

Ever since we were children, my mother has always reacted badly to pressure, particularly concerning deadlines. Her father was partly to blame for this, having brought her up on the maxim 'Time was made for slaves'. She is perfectly willing to put herself out for other people, but in her own time. Somehow she always manages to make herself late, almost as if to say defiantly, 'You can't control me!'. Occasionally, when by some fluke she is ready ahead of time and looks dangerously likely to be prompt for a rehearsal or a rendezvous, she will rectify this threatening situation in her own very individual way. She gathers up all the paper that cannot be recycled, takes it to the end of her garden and lights a bonfire that burns too furiously to be abandoned. Unfortunately, the inevitable pressure created by the realization that she is now going to be late, has – and always has had – alarming manifestations for those around her. The whole house is sent into turmoil, and we are all to blame. Her things have mysteriously developed legs and taken themselves into far corners of the house. We are all shouted at and shrieked at and cursed and accused. To say that my mother has never played Lady Macbeth is a lie. I have seen her play it many times in her life – usually in the kitchen! Years ago I tried to develop ways of helping her through these dramas. Getting angry as well was a complete failure, and could be very dangerous. Eventually I found that to keep very calm and always be a few steps ahead of her was the answer.

'Who has hidden my gloves?'

'Here they are.'

'I knew it was a mistake to have my coat cleaned.'

'I picked it up from the dry cleaners yesterday. And, by the way, here are your car keys. I've warmed up the engine and your bag with the script is already in the car.'

Frustrated and dumbfounded by the lack of a drama she reaches for the waste-paper basket – it's empty.

'Where's the rubbish? I hadn't sorted it out yet.'

'I had a bonfire this morning when you were shopping.'

'There were things in there that were not meant to be burnt.'

'I took them out.'

'Where are they?'

Difficult – it was no good pretending that the dustmen had come that day if they hadn't; and, quite honestly, I would not have put it past her to have chased down to the rubbish depot to salvage her recyclable paper. 'I've hidden them somewhere where you can't find them and I refuse to tell you where until tonight when you come home. You don't have time to sort them out now – you'll be late for rehearsal.'

'I'm always on time when other people aren't around.' (I wonder.)

'There is absolutely no reason for you to be late now. You are ready – there is nothing to burn. Will you *please* go.'

'But the dogs ...'

'The dogs are fine, and they will be a lot better when this place has calmed down after you've gone!'

All the family had gone to endless pains to make quite sure that her very special day went smoothly. She was the star, and was to be pampered and cosseted. Unlike many actresses, my mothers buys few clothes and when she does she prefers to be casual and comfortable; purchasing something to wear to Buckingham Palace had not been an easy task. My sister and I helped to dress her in the carefully selected outfit. How we had agonized over the skirt, the hat, the blouse! The neighbours arrived to check out her finery; she very seldom dresses up. The dogs could not understand what was happening, and took out their frustrations by frantically barking at the birds that had landed on her garden table to eat their daily helping of Kenwood-processed crusts.

This was the one day when we could not be late. The question was should we leave early to avoid the dreaded London traffic, or were we better to leave a little late, when the worst of the traffic was over? Once again we agonized. Having decided that it was best to leave after the traffic, all our plans were nearly foiled by the extremely untimely arrival of a delivery van, whose driver would not be put off, despite our earnest disclosures that we were off to 'The Palace'. His truck was parked across the front gate, and he would not move it until he had delivered the wood for the fence and been paid for it. (The old fence had been blown down by the recent hurricane.)

So, just when she should have been splashing on that last drop of Chanel No.5 or securing 'the hat' against the wind, my mother was struggling to find glasses and cheque books in that well known phenomenon 'the other handbag'.

Fortunately, the journey to the Palace was traffic-free. When we arrived, in good time, we were lined up in what looked like the start to a mini-Grand Prix, opposite the entrance to the Palace gates, which were duly opened at the stroke of 10 a.m. Official entry passes were shown at the gate. Finally we were there – in the Holy of Holies – the Palace's interior courtyard. A highly trained bomb squad examined all the cars and when everything had been meticulously checked, we were allowed into the Palace itself.

The grandeur of Buckingham Palace was all we'd expected, and more. Ornate ceilings, with their cornices picked out in gold leaf, were supported by the noblest marble pillars. There were statues, magnificent paintings, priceless furniture and ornaments. Brass-plated guardsmen gleamed as they stood to attention in the vestibule.

At this point, the recipients of awards were diverted up a separate staircase from their guests, so we kissed my mother, wished her good luck, and followed in the footsteps of those in front of us to the Ballroom where the investiture ceremony was to take place. We were then seated on red plush benches directly beneath the organ loft, where a military band was rather half-heartedly playing some songs from the shows. The whole operation was discreetly but superbly regimented by the welcoming members of the Palace staff.

My mother, meanwhile, went with the other recipients to a large hall, where they were soon briefed on the forthcoming procedures by a light-hearted member of the Palace staff, whose job was obviously to relax the award-winners, as well as to put them through their paces. He reassured them that anything that could possibly go wrong, such as collapsing in an undignified heap at the feet of Her Majesty, had already happened a thousand times before. Everything was done to make them feel comfortable, and that is the only explanation possible for the selection of music that had been chosen for the occasion. For example, after the Yeomen of the Guard had marched in (a comedy routine that would have fitted well into any Danny Kaye movie) and taken up their positions on the dais in the Ballroom, the band struck up with 'A Spoonful of Sugar Makes the Medicine Go Down!' Later, during the dubbing of one of England's newest knights, the band reduced some of us to muffled laughter with a rendering of 'Consider Yourself Well In, Consider Yourself One Of The Family.'

The ceremony itself was an emotional experience. We rose to our feet as instructed, at the entrance of a page, then – as we held our breath – the Queen herself entered the Ballroom, a people's Queen, no crown or robes. She wore a pale gold silk suit decorated with the most exquisite brooch, she had no hat or gloves. Her behaviour was relaxed and natural, and her face radiated her obvious good nature. 'God Save the Queen' was sung, and then the Queen proceeded to endow all the hundred and twenty recipients with their various knight-hoods, orders and decorations for bravery.

My mother, being a highly skilled performer, took it all in her stride, seeming to relish every moment. It was the culmination of a lifetime of devotion to the theatre; she had earned it and she was determined to enjoy her day. After the ceremony was all over, and we were taking photographs in the courtyard, a man approached my mother and said, 'I am delighted to see you win this very well-deserved award; you must be extremely proud.'

'I am enormously proud,' replied my mother, 'but it is not I who should be receiving it. The person who should have had this award is my father, George Frederick Hayes, who spent all his life enduring a really boring job, in order that I should be able to have my career.'

1
Origins

George Frederick Hayes, my grandfather, was born in 1884, in a sleepy Irish country town called Ballintubber, in County Cork. Always known as Sus, he had an older brother, Bill, a sister, Minnie, and a younger brother, Frank. Their father, also George, always referred to himself (even on his passport) as a Gentleman Farmer; but there was no farm. He had been left enough money after the sale of the family flour mill to maintain his family, but as far as my mother can remember her grandfather never went to work. The Hayes were of the Protestant ascendancy, for Cork had once been a stronghold of Ireland's English Protestant rulers. They were generous and charitable, but made it clear to their children that they were not to befriend any Catholics.

Kathleen Hayes, née O'Callaghan, Sus's mother, was a beauty and a tower of strength, enjoying her four children and life in the grand old home at Ballintubber. My mother visited the house quite recently and explained to the current owner that her father used to live there, and with true Irish hospitality she was welcomed in and allowed to look around the house she had heard so much about as a child.

Growing up in Ireland in my grandfather's youth was very different from life today. The children had a blissfully happy childhood, running wild through the beautiful countryside, building dams in the streams, collecting blackberries and bringing them home to be made into delicious jam. Sus and his friends had wonderful adventures in the long summers, swimming across Dead Man's Gulch to Queenstown Island where they would have great battles with the Catholic boys.

His sister Minnie was rather delicate and spent a lot of time at home. Kathleen, who knew everyone and had friends everywhere, provided all the excitement and entertainment Minnie needed. They spent hours together discussing books they had read, choosing materials for their dresses and planning delicious menus. They were not wealthy, but, like so many people in those days, they had servants. Minnie lived at home until her mother died; when asked why she had not married, she would reply that she was much too happy at home with Mud, her mother.

The older boys went off to school at Middleton College, where they were known as Hayes Major and Minor – indeed, Bill was to remain 'Major' for the rest of his life. Middleton College was seven miles from home, and they drove themselves there with the jennet (a female donkey) and trap every day, through all types of weather, unless it was snowing or the jennet was lame. Then they would walk!

In those days there were three choices of career for boys of their class: the Church, the Bank or the Civil Service. The Church did not appeal to my grandfather. Eventually his parents were summoned to Middleton College, and told that he was too bright to work in the Bank. They were recommended to send him to a college originally founded to educate poor Catholic boys, and run by the Christian Brothers in Cork City; there he would pass the Civil Service examinations and be able to get himself a better job, maybe even in England.

That distant prospect delighted his parents, particularly the thought that he was far more likely to meet a nice Protestant girl in England.

So off he went to the Christian Brothers, with strict instructions that he was to be kind to everyone, but never make friends with Catholic boys because they were not to be trusted. On his first visit home he informed his parents that the Catholic boys at the college, though poor, were extremely honest and he much preferred them! How worried his parents must have been, longing for the day when he would be safely in England.

The Christian Brothers believed in very strict discipline; nowadays they might even be called cruel, because they would not tolerate laziness, lateness or bad behaviour, and any wayward boys were beaten frequently. Sus, however, was a clever and diligent student who applied himself enthusiastically to his studies and was a keen sportsman. He had a delightful sunny nature and a most rare sense of humour that made him extremely popular with everyone. My mother says that no man in her life ever matched up to her father. We, his grandchildren, all adored him too.

He passed his examinations and duly sailed for England, where he stayed with his grandmother who lived in London until he found his feet. She lived in the Brixton area, where he knew no one; but he discovered he could meet other Irish boys at the local Catholic church on Sundays, where they should have been at Mass but were, more likely, smoking outside during the service. He met a group of young people and in no time at all was roped in to perform in the Christmas pantomime put on by the Catholic Social Club. He played a fireman. It was here that he met Florence Lawler, an Irish Catholic!

Florence Lawler, my grandmother, was born in London of Irish parents in 1886; according to her birth certificate, though it looks suspiciously as if she may have altered the date from 1881! Her parents had married and run away to England where they had five daughters, Lizzie, Kitty, Molly, Agnes and Florence, the baby.

Tragically, her mother died when Florence was only one year old. Her father could not bring up the five girls on his own, so the older four were sent into care in the convent, but little Florence was handed over to a childless second cousin, Aunt Rose, and her husband Charles Joseph.

Aunt Rose knew little about bringing up children. Even though she was not her own child, she could not understand why Florence did not immediately fall in with her plans and be obedient and co-operative. Her idea of having a little girl was to dress her up like a doll and take her out for drives sitting next to her in the carriage. Her sisters used to see her drive past and feel envious, wishing that they too could live in such luxury.

Aunt Rose was extremely strict, to the point of cruelty – after all, they were still living in Victorian times. She seemed to want to deny Florence anything that would bring her pleasure. Florence became able to keep complete control over her facial expressions, to show no enthusiasm or delight, because the minute Aunt Rose saw delight on her face, its cause would be removed.

One night, the maid who had been looking after Florence during the day related a charming incident to Aunt Rose on her return. Apparently 'Little Florence' had been playing the piano with her toes! Aunt Rose did not find it charming or amusing, but immediately flew into a towering rage and dragged the sleeping five-year-old from her bed to give her a hard beating.

Florence had a very unhappy childhood, being reared by someone incapable of showing her affection, whose idea of love seemed to be harsh discipline and punishments. Her life would have been intolerable had it not been for Uncle Charles, her stepfather, who found in this pretty little creature a great joy and loved her independent spirit and sharp wit. He was a scholarly Jew who dealt in precious stones, and it was due to his kindness that, all through her life, my grandmother would never hear a bad word against the Jews.

Florence's real father used to visit the house regularly, whereupon the whisky bottle would come out. He was a heavy drinker and, when he was in his cups, he would sit Florence on his lap and give her a gold sovereign. As soon as he had sobered up he would ask her for the money back! His drinking, and that of some of Aunt Rose's other friends, left a deep impression on my grandmother who hated alcohol all her life.

Aunt Rose had been a dancer for a while; there is no way to trace her experiences but, whatever they were, she was determined that Florence should not go on the stage. This created the seeds of my mother's career. A frustrated actress herself, my grandmother was to encourage all her children into the theatre from a very early age.

Florence herself was taught to sing and play the piano. She was very gifted and would be called downstairs to the drawing-room when Aunt Rose was entertaining, to perform for the guests. She told us that she contracted diphtheria during her early years (it was quite common in those days, before a vaccine was discovered) and she was devastated to find that her voice had lost some of its quality.

The Catholic Notre-Dame Convent was chosen for her education. The nuns were a Belgian order, very old-fashioned and narrow-minded. Fortunately there was one nun, Sister Mechtild, who thought the world of Florence. She asked her to become a pupil-teacher at the age of fourteen.

A pupil-teacher used to sit in the teacher's desk, making sure that the girls in the class did their studies, answering any questions or queries they might have. From this early age she became, and always was, an excellent teacher. She was responsible for my mother's good diction and command of the English language.

Encouraged by her sister Molly, Florence left home when she was sixteen to go to Teacher Training College. She never returned home, and Aunt Rose never forgave her. Aunt Rose would not allow her to see Uncle Charles on his death-bed and, consequently, Florence refused to visit Aunt Rose when she was dying and asked for her.

The Teacher Training College was called St Charles', and was run by nuns of the Sacred Heart, who were progressive and, above all, fairminded. Many of them were the daughters of the Catholic aristocracy. However, it was still the Victorian era. The young ladies were discouraged from any temptation to be vain; they were not even allowed to take a bath in the nude but had to wear a long chemise. One girl who had extremely beautiful hair used to wash it secretly at night in cold water. Eventually she became very ill with a glandular disease caused by lying in bed in the freezing cold with her wet hair on a damp pillow. A very prim nun told them a cautionary story about another girl who had beautiful hair. Apparently this girl went to a party during the school holidays, at which a young man who was talking to her ran his fingers through her hair. 'She did not say anything,' said the nun. 'But she looked at him – straight – and he knew that he had gone too far!'

During the holidays, my grandmother stayed with her eldest sister, Lizzie, who already had her own home. She had been married very young to a bookmaker, who later inherited a laundry. He had no time to run the laundry so Lizzie took it over and, despite the fact that she went on to have six children, she made a huge success of it. (Indeed, it is still in the family now.) Lizzie was a truly remarkable woman. Her family used to say in fun that, on her one day off, she would go to the cinema with four knitting needles and a ball of wool and would leave, having watched the film, carrying a pair of socks.

When Uncle Charles died he left no money, for he inherited nothing from his family because he did not marry a Jew. It was Lizzie who provided for Aunt Rose, allowing her to live in a house that she owned in Clacton.

Lizzie's children were Charles, Ambrose, Betty, Marjorie, Gerard and Teddy, but when Florence was staying with her she had only the first two boys. Florence adored them; and maybe that was the time when she discovered her preference for teaching boys. She qualified as a teacher at a very early age and, since her qualification was the most basic, she always taught in what were called Elementary schools. These schools provided a free education for the children of poorer backgrounds, who could not afford to pay for their education.

Florence always preferred to teach boys, and she was extremely good at it. She managed to teach some of the older boys to read, after they had slipped through the net, working with them slowly and laboriously, never letting them get away until she was quite sure that they really could read. Years later, many of these boys would make a special trip back to the school to thank her; perhaps after receiving promotion that they would never have achieved without the ability to read.

My grandmother told many delightful stories, which we loved to hear, about her teaching days. One concerned a boy called Gorman. He was probably the slowest boy in the class, maybe a little retarded, but very conscientious. Once a month the boys had to go to confession, and on this day Gorman was kneeling in one of the church pews, examining his conscience rather noisily. Verbatim he was heard to say in his gruff Cockney voice, 'Sauced me muvver. Give Dempsey a punch on the nose,' and then the grand finale, 'Shoved a gas-pipe down a drain 'ole!'

Florence, for some reason, was the most terrible snob. All through my mother's childhood, she and her brother and sister were never allowed to mention the fact that their mother was a teacher, because she only taught at Elementary schools. They had to say that their mother went to 'the office'.

Once Florence had qualified and started teaching she went to live with a large family called Williams, where she was extremely happy. While she was there, she joined the local Catholic Social Club and there she met George F. Hayes, known to all as Sus. Shortly after they met, they started courting. He used to visit her on his bicycle. She rode a bicycle too – it was the best form of transport. Her only problem was that she could not mount or dismount on her own; there had to be someone to help her on as she set off, and someone to catch her at the other end.

Eventually my grandfather wrote home to his mother in Ireland: 'I have met a delightful Irish girl out here, and I intend to marry her.'

'I'm delighted to hear about the wonderful Irish girl,' wrote his mother. 'I hope she's a Protestant.'

He replied on a postcard by return of post. 'I hope she's not!'

It must have been an awful shock to the Hayes family, and a great disappointment, particularly as he was the only one of the children to have a family, which meant that all their grandchildren were Catholics. When finally he took Florence home to meet the in-laws they loved her and treated her with enormous affection, but they never invited any of their friends around to meet her.

Sus was in complete agreement that any children should be brought up as Catholics, and therefore he had to take instruction in the faith before they were married. He went to a local priest, Canon Menane, and they got on extremely well; in fact, in years to come, if the children had any queries about the religion, it was always their father that they went to, although he never became a Catholic. Years later he re-met Canon Menane at a church bazaar and they were deep in conversation for a long time. Apparently the Canon was amazed to find that Sus had never converted. Sus explained that he would have found it very difficult while his mother was alive. It was a matter of loyalty to the family. Speaking of loyalty: a nun once suggested to my mother that they should pray for her poor father to become a Catholic. She was told, very smartly, that her Daddy was absolutely perfect as he was and the nun quickly said, 'Well, we must thank God then that you have such a wonderful Daddy.'

The young couple were married in August 1908 from the Williams' house. It was a small wedding, mainly family and a few close friends. They went to Cliftonville for their honeymoon, and after their return moved into a flat in Camberwell. The rent they paid was about five shillings a week.

Unfortunately, soon after they were married, Sus contracted measles, quite a dangerous disease in those days. He developed complications and as a result he gradually began to lose his hearing. They say it is an ill wind that blows no good, because it is very likely that my mother's ability to project could be partly due to years of raising her voice so that her father would not be left out of the family conversations.

In December 1909, Florence gave birth to their first-born, a girl, christened Patricia Lawler Hayes. And so the story really begins ...

2

A Child's Talent

Patricia weighed the same at three months as she had at birth. Florence could not breast-feed, and Patricia was unable to digest cows' milk. The doctor made it quite clear that unless drastic action was taken the baby was going to die. He recommended that she be sent back to the nursing-home where she had been born, to be looked after by a wonderful nurse called Sister Reeve. 'If anyone can save her, she can.'

Sister Reeve worked miracles and, leaving Patricia in her expert care, Florence went back to work. My mother stayed in the nursing-home until she was eight months old. Then her parents took her to Ireland for the summer holidays. On their return she went back to Sister Reeve until the birth of her sister Moira, in April 1911, when she returned home with her mother and the new-born baby.

The following period was very traumatic for all concerned. My mother had been beautifully looked after by Sister Reeve, who was highly organized and very skilled at taking care of babies. My grandmother on the other hand was not at all domesticated; she never had a great deal of physical energy, and she just muddled along. Her own unhappy childhood had left its scars and she found it difficult to relax and enjoy her first two children.

The early separation from her mother affected Patricia all her life. Their relationship was always difficult, although they loved one another, and she was extremely jealous of Moira –

and even more so of Brian, who was born in April 1912, by which time Florence was ready to enjoy a baby, particularly a boy.

However, Brian was very delicate and Florence had the same feeding problems. One day Patricia asked her mother, 'Why is baby brother going to die?'

Apparently some friend who had seen him in his crib looking pale and fragile had been heard by my mother whispering, 'He looks so frail I think he's going to die.'

There seems to have been a lot more ill health in those days. The Hayes family had all the childhood diseases, most of them severely, and poor Sus, who had escaped them in his youth in Ireland, caught them one by one from his children. Eventually the whole family was desperately ill with scarlet fever, which in those days was a notifiable disease. The authorities insisted on fumigating the house after they had recovered; and my grandmother maintained that following the fumigation they had far fewer colds and influenza.

Florence was very possessive of her children. They were seldom allowed out to play, and she always made a point of disliking any of their friends – often on the grounds that they were 'common and did not speak properly'.

However, as far as their education was concerned there was no criticism of Florence's attitude. As soon as Patricia could talk, my grandmother began teaching her nursery rhymes. She was not allowed to gabble them in a meaningless way like most children, all rhythm and no understanding, but had to enunciate them clearly and boldly, as if she was on a large stage with an audience. She was sent to a little dame-school when she was three years old and, due to the grounding she had received at home, she learned to read almost immediately.

It was at this very early age that Florence began to teach Patricia to recite poetry. My mother clearly remembers standing at her mother's knee in the kitchen while she recited her a poem called 'The Lamplighter', by Robert Louis Stevenson. It is about a little boy watching Leary the lamplighter pass by at dusk. He hopes that when he grows up he may light the lamps with Leary. When Florence had finished the poem, my mother burst into uncontrollable sobs. 'Mummy, it's so sad.' At that tiny age she was overwhelmed by the power of the spoken word.

Florence and Sus were never very well off while their children were young; his diminishing hearing prevented him from being promoted in the Civil Service. However, they were both earning; and they somehow managed to find the money for private education and to spend every holiday – Christmas, Easter and summer – at the seaside. Florence loved the freedom of being able to send all three children down to the beach to play; in those days they were completely safe. The only unexpected thing that happened was that my mother thought she saw a ghost one day, a very old-fashioned lady who walked past them and then vanished. Another day they went down to the water to have a swim and when they returned it was to see the last of Moira's white lace petticoat disappearing into a goat's mouth.

A popular elocution teacher, who lived near the family in Streatham, also had a flat in Littlehampton. This seemed to be absolutely ideal since the Hayes family had rented a holiday flat on the sea-front in Littlehampton on a permanent basis. All the children began their dancing and elocution lessons with Olive Richardson. Richie, as she was known, was aware straight away of Patricia's talent and felt that she had an up-and-coming star in the making.

Looking back, Richie's methods were very affected and 'stagey', excellent for a shy child who needed bringing out, but rather over the top for Patricia. However, she taught my mother some of the pieces that she still moves us to tears with today, such as Prince Arthur's speech from *King John*, 'Hubert must you with hot irons burn out both mine eyes?' and 'Froggie Face', a little French girl talking about a little English boy she met on an English beach in the First World War.

My mother studied with Olive Richardson for many years. She used to win all the talent contests which were held at the

seaside during the summer months with her dramatic ren-
derings, and learned very quickly the amazing power that she
had over an audience. Imagine going to a seaside talent contest
and finding yourself moved to tears by a tiny six-year-old
giving a powerful rendition of 'The murder of Nancy' from
Oliver Twist!

Patricia began to have money of her own that she had won,
and which was always placed in a Post Office account. She
realized very early on the independence that having your own
money will give you.

The *Daily Mail* regularly held sandbuilding competitions.
The children would build a picture with sand, seaweed and
stones; these would be judged by a panel and the winners
would receive money prizes. One summer, when the family
were at Broadstairs, my mother came third in the contest and
was very disappointed. She noticed that the competition
moved to Ramsgate the following week and when she told her
father that she had had a good idea, he agreed to take her to
Ramsgate on the bus. Her plan was to draw a donkey on her
allotted space on the sand, fill in the outline with crumbled
chalk, then write in stones surrounded by green seaweed:
'Poor Donkey he can't read the *Daily Mail*'

' "This Ass does not read the *Daily Mail*" might be even
better,' her father suggested.

She won the first prize of £3.15s (£3.75), a big amount in
those days. She bought herself a bicycle.

When Patricia was eleven, J.B. Fagan – a famous actor and
entrepreneur – was travelling around various children's acting
schools looking for talent. He saw Patricia at Olive Richardson's and hired her to play a little girl in his production of *The
Great Big World* by Katherine Barnsley with music by Franco
Leoni. It was based on all the characters out of the popular
children's comic *Rainbow*. My mother was to play Molly, the
only girl in a family of boys. When Molly appeared as an adult
in the third act, my mother played her own five-year-old son
Mark! This could have been the start of her famous reputation
for playing boys, which continued until quite recently.

It is interesting to note that Miles Malleson, who was to become such a famous character actor, played Slim Jim and Tiger Tim in the production (which was at the Court Theatre). Moreover, Olive Richardson herself also played a small part, probably in order that she could be around to keep an eye on all her little fledglings!

To obtain an actor's licence in those days a child had to be twelve years old. The play was due to open on 18 December 1921, but had to be postponed until the 26th because Patricia was not twelve until 22 December. She received some excellent reviews, and luckily my grandmother kept them.

> ... notably little Patricia Hayes who thus early in her 12th year has already the charm and self-possession of an accomplished actress
>
> *Daily Telegraph*

> ... Patricia Hayes who although only just of age to appear before the footlights shows promise of a career
>
> *News of the World*

> ... The most remarkable thing about the production is the acting of Patricia Hayes, here is truly remarkable evidence of a child's talent
>
> *Birmingham Post*

There were many more, all equally admiring of her shining ability.

When Patricia was fifteen years old, Olive Richardson sent her to see an agent called Bernhardt and he cast her as the boy lead 'Tyl-Tyl' in *The Bluebird*, a famous play by the Belgian playwright Maurice Maeterlinck. Two children are searching for the Bluebird of Happiness. They finally find it after many adventures, right there in their own home. Once again she received wonderful notices for her remarkable performance.

Moira was also in the play as one of the lost children, and as a bat. Her great joy was that as the bat she had to fly, which she has always treasured as a marvellous experience. Florence went off on tour with her two daughters, while their father stayed at home and looked after Brian. They toured Edinburgh, Cardiff, Bournemouth, Southampton, Bristol, Glasgow and Manchester. Sixty years later Moira remembered all the venues quite clearly.

Unfortunately, in Edinburgh, my mother was taken ill. At first it was thought she had influenza. Then she developed a very stiff neck. Everyone was very concerned about her, even her Scottish landlady said, 'This child should not be allowed to perform, she's got the lumps.'

It was the mumps. The manager begged Florence to let Patricia do the opening night, so, despite her indisposition, she struggled on. Apparently, while she was on stage acting she was fine, but as soon as she came off stage, tears from the pain would be pouring down her face. She missed the next two performances and her pay was docked.

History repeated itself years later, when my sister Gemma was touring with my mother in a play called *Relative Values*. Poor Gemma too became very ill with mumps. She was so ill, in fact, that she had to abandon the tour.

One summer, the Hayes children met another family, the Darnboroughs, at Littlehampton. The children were called Hermione and Tony. Mr Darnborough was one of only two men who had ever broken the bank of Monte Carlo, and he'd made an absolute fortune. Needless to say, like most gamblers he gradually lost a lot of it. He was a representative for an unusual and prestigious American car called the Paige. My mother remembers him as a charming and very generous man from the States. His wife Frances was very highly connected, a society belle, elegant and beautiful. She was the only person my mother ever recalls to hold her face rigid if you made her laugh. 'Don't make me laugh,' she would say. 'I'll get wrinkles!'

It has already been mentioned that my grandmother was a tremendous snob – she liked this association between the two families and they became very friendly with the Darnboroughs who 'spoke well, and were anything but common'. Frances Darnborough encouraged Florence to take the children away from Olive Richardson and send them to 'a good school' of acting and dancing. 'Patricia is very talented. Send her to Euphan McClaren's, where Hermione goes,' she said.

As soon as they returned to London, my grandmother visited the McClaren's and from then on Patricia and Moira attended the school (which was also a theatrical management). Twice weekly, after ordinary school, they made their way across from Streatham to High Street Kensington by public transport to do arduous ballet exercises. My mother tried hard at ballet, without much pleasure or any success, but once again she excelled in the acting classes.

Shortly after she started with the McClaren's they sent her to see a producer called William Poel. He was a great Shakespeare specialist, President of the Shakespeare League, and interested in reviving the original Elizabethan productions. When my mother saw him he was going to put on an all-boy production of *Julius Caesar*. He was looking for boys who could play Shakespeare, so imagine his surprise when Patricia turned up at the auditions! He felt sorry for her because she had travelled right across London to see him, and agreed to let her recite her pieces. She recited Viola's speech from *Twelfth Night*: 'I left no ring with her, what means this lady?'; and Cassius' speech to Brutus from *Julius Caesar*:

> 'I know that virtue to be in you, Brutus,
> As well as I do know your outward
> favour.'

When she had finished, William Poel said, 'You have a most remarkable talent for Shakespeare. I shall certainly use you in the play – no one will ever know you are not a boy!' (Unfortunately it did not happen; William Poel fell ill and the production never took place.)

Mathesson Lang, the great actor/director, contacted the McClaren's. He wanted my mother to understudy a girl called Elsie Judge in *Grand Hotel* by Vicki Baum, which he was taking on tour. Patricia and Elsie had to travel around the country with a chaperone. They were very happy on the tour, for Mathesson Lang adored the two girls and made a big fuss of them. When Patricia was eighteen, Mathesson Lang sent for her to cast her in another play he was putting on. However, when he saw her, he said, 'Oh dear, I thought you would be a big girl by now, but you don't look eighteen. This is a play about a girl who is being forced to marry a man she does not like. I'm afraid we need someone more mature.'

Peggy Ashcroft got the part and she never looked back, says my mother!

Patricia, Moira and Brian all attended a local convent, Coventry Hall, for their formal education. Until he was seven, Brian was in the special boys' department run by Mother Mary Alice, who was very strict but she loved her boys. By and large, though, the nuns of Coventry Hall were very old-fashioned and prim. Patricia and Moira were not encouraged to show their acting talents although occasionally Moira, a gifted writer, would write a play with the leading part for Patricia, and they would be allowed to perform it for Reverend Mother's Feast.

My mother was going to recite a poem one open day but came to school with a button missing from her shoe. When she admitted that she had forgotten to replace the button, she was not allowed to recite the poem. What a horrible punishment for a gifted child! My mother says, 'It did not teach me that I must remember to sew my buttons on, but it did teach me that in life I must watch out for mean-hearted people!'

During the tour of *Grand Hotel* my mother missed some school. Sister Aloysia, the headmistress, wrote to my grandmother and asked her to remove Patricia from the school, because 'a girl who is going to be an actress will not be a good influence on the other girls. Moira, however, may remain at the school.'

Florence, filled with just anger, went straight to a school in Wandsworth called West Hill, run by the Sacred Heart nuns,

and saw the headmistress, Mother Burnett. 'Send both
Patricia and Moira here,' said Mother Burnett. 'We will be
delighted to have them.' Brian was then at Wimbledon
College, the well-known Jesuit School to which my brother
Richard went, and also much more recently my own son
Tom.

Mathesson Lang advised Florence to send Patricia to
RADA's classes for sixteen- to eighteen-year-olds. She
attended school in the mornings and went to RADA in the
afternoons. This continued for a year, until her father decided
she should concentrate solely on passing her final school
examinations.

The two years my mother spent at the Sacred Heart
Convent, West Hill, were very happy ones. She encountered
there the best teacher anyone could hope to have, a Miss Ivy
Ashlin. She often wonders what became of her. 'She couldn't
teach me to be good at mathematics, but it became my
favourite subject.'

Both Moira and Patricia were greatly encouraged at West
Hill; they were put in charge of all school plays, many of
which were written by Moira.

Having passed her exams Patricia went back to RADA on
a full-time basis. Celia Johnson was also there, but only in the
French classes. My mother says that she was very gifted and
beautiful: a typical English rose, she seemed to step straight
out of RADA into a brilliant career.

Patricia went into the final year and at the end of the
second term the Public Show was to be held, at which the
coveted Bancroft Gold Medal would be awarded. Can you
imagine the anticipation with which she rushed to the
notice-board to see which parts she had been cast in for the
Special Performance, which was to be judged by Sir Gerald
du Maurier, Edith Evans and Frank Cellier?

There on the notice-board she saw with glee that she had
been cast in three plays. She was to be Fanny in *Hindle
Wakes* by Stanley Houghton, Petya, Natasha's younger
brother, in Tolstoy's *War and Peace* and a beggar-woman in

a mimed version of *Don Juan* (The last two productions were to be by Komisarjevsky, the great Russia director, who had been quick to notice Patricia's talent and insisted on having her in both his productions.)

Helen Haye, a well-known actress of the day, was going to direct *Hindle Wakes*. At the first rehearsal, Helen Haye said to my mother, 'The part of Fanny needs a big woman, which you are not; so I am going to speak to Mr Barnes.'

Later Mr Barnes, the Principal, told my grandmother: 'I had a terrible battle to get Helen to let Patricia play the part. She did not think she was right for it. I said, "I take your point, but I have cast Patricia in it. Rehearse her for one week and if you are not pleased with her, then I will remove her and you can recast the part." '

At the end of the week no more was said.

Helen Haye was very strict at rehearsals; she never unbent towards my mother, never showed any pleasure or encouragement. When it came to the day of the Public Show and the curtain went up, she sat in the wings in the dark and listened. At the end of the scene, Fanny breaks down, bursts into tears and makes an exit crying, slamming the door as she goes.

As she walked through the wings in the darkness to tremendous applause, a hand came out and grabbed my mother's hand very hard and shook it fiercely. That was the only sign Helen Haye ever gave of her approval.

After her performance as the beggar-woman in *Don Juan* Patricia felt a little hungry and slipped up the road to get a cup of tea and a bun. When she returned, all her friends gathered around her in a state of amazement, asking, 'Where have you been? *You have won the Gold Medal*!'

The announcement had been made and there had been no sign of the winner. Mr Barnes, the Principal, greeted her with, 'Well, thank goodness you are back. Congratulations, you have won the Gold Medal. *Now you have got to grow!*'

3

Repertory Theatre

'I won the Gold Medal at RADA, and spent the next eighteen months out of work.'

My mother was very immature at eighteen. My grandmother had never encouraged her to 'grow up', always trying to keep her children young and innocent. Even when my brother and I were children, and my mother was expecting her third child, my grandmother begged her not to take away our innocence when we questioned her about the new brother or sister who was growing inside her. A great friend of Patricia's, who had become a nun, commented, 'You are not taking away their innocence, you are taking away their ignorance.'

Poor Florence had had no mother of her own to teach her about life and she did not begin to understand about presentation in the very difficult task of getting work. Patricia was sent off to auditions in home-made clothes that very often did not suit her. And yet Florence imagined that every film and stage producer would immediately be clamouring for my mother's services. After she had won the Gold Medal there was a lot of publicity in the newspapers, and Peter Hodge, who was running BBC Children's Hour, telephoned her and asked her to come up that afternoon to read a story.

From then on, until Children's Hour was done away with (needlessly, she felt), the BBC always gave her a certain amount of work every year. In the early days of radio, it was necessary for actors to have their wits about them for these broadcasts. Frequently she would receive a message in the morning asking her to come in in the afternoon to be in a play. During the read-through the producer might say, 'I'm sorry, the last two pages aren't written yet. We will start the broadcast at 5.15 and they will be ready for you before you've finished.' There were no recordings then; all radio was live. Half way through the programme she would be handed two more pages. They would reach the end of the part they had prepared and read the rest completely unrehearsed.

There cannot be many actors who remember such hair-raising times. A few of the names from those days are the late Ivan Sampson, Norman Shelley and Carlton Hobbs, who was reputed to have kept every single contract and script that he had received since he started working for the BBC.

Apart from a small amount of radio work, Patricia was unemployed for eighteen months. Finally, she was offered a ten-week season with J.B. Fagan's repertory company, the Oxford Players. They put on a season of plays at the Oxford Playhouse during the university terms, and were frequently directed by an excellent producer called Claud Gurney. My mother says he taught her some very important lessons at this critical, early stage in her career. For example, she was once performing in a Strindberg one-acter in which she and a young man were having a conversation. There was a hyacinth in a pot on the table next to them. During the course of the play the young man had to say, 'Isn't that hyacinth beautiful?'

'Yes – it's an image of the cosmos,' responded my mother, with great feeling, a reply that occasioned a shriek of laughter from the audience which 'completely flummoxed' her.

After the performance Claud Gurney congratulated her, but she said, 'It was horrible, they were laughing at me. Laughing when I was quite serious.'

Claud Gurney decided to call a short rehearsal with the two actors the next day, to show them how to cope with the situation. 'When you have a line like that, one that could be suspect, you must treat it as if it is insignificant and the other person must come in very quickly with the next line.' This trick has stood her in good stead for many a year.

She played Dolly in *You Never Can Tell*, and on the first night got tremendous laughs on every line. The second night she went on confidently relishing the thought of the hilariously funny part she was playing. There were practically no laughs at all.

'Tonight they were an awful audience,' she complained to Mr Gurney.

'Never blame an audience – it is always your fault if they do not laugh. I'm not blaming you, because you are inexperienced. I could take you through your part line by line, and show you how to get the laughs, but that would spoil your spontaneity ... This is the secret: if you yourself think it's funny, the audience won't. If you expect them to laugh, they won't. You must play it for the truth of it, and if it is funny they will laugh. I'm afraid the rest is a matter of experience.'

It is hardly surprising to learn that Patricia has always been interested in getting laughs. She remarked that once you have worked with the comedians, a laugh is more important than anything else. The famous director Ron Eyre was once annoyed with her because, when asked to change what she was doing in a scene, she said, 'But if I do it like that, I won't get a laugh.'

'Who says you *should* get a laugh? Play it for real, and the laughs will come.'

In a letter to her mother from the Oxford Playhouse, Patricia wrote:

Mr Gurney says they always laugh at serious plays at Oxford, and that once, when they did *Heartbreak House* and the author, Bernard Shaw, was in front, they laughed and laughed, and afterwards called for Shaw, who eventually gave them a scathing lecture!

Here is another delightful extract from a letter written to her mother at that time. But in this case she is not so concerned with her acting.

Now I come to the most amusing part of my letter. On Saturday night the Commissionaire came round to the dressing-room with a card on which was the name Mr Dudley Fleming – and an address – The Vicarage, Tyldesley, Nr. Manchester. He asked me if I would see the gentleman and said that he was told to mention RADA and I would remember. Well, I seemed to know the name, and as everyone appeared very impressed about my having an 'admirer' from the front – I went down. This was after the first act of *To Have The Honour*.

I remembered the face when I saw him; he was in the A's or the Middles when I was in the Finals (at RADA), and he told me that he saw me in the Public Show, and that as soon as he recognized my name on the programme he dashed around to see me. Of course I was very honoured and all that, and then he asked if he could take me out to tea one afternoon. I said I was very busy rehearsing but that he had better come to the show some day next week and then he could come round again. Imagine my surprise when I came off after the first act last night to find him standing in the corridor! He said he was enjoying the play enormously, and I said I was sorry he had come for the first performance because everything was going so badly. He said,

'May I take you out to tea tomorrow?' I said, 'Yes, if there isn't a rehearsal, I'd love to come, but I can't let you know until the morning.' Then he presented me with some chocolates and went away. But ... that isn't all.

After the last act, the commissionaire came around with another card on which was written 'Can I see you some time this evening? – Michael Barnsley – "The Great Big World" – St John's Cottage.'

Of course I knew who this was – Mrs Barnsley's son – the youngest one. I told the Commissionaire that I'd see him after the show – the dressing-room was still more impressed!

So, when the show was over, I went behind and found a young man – or rather a youth – who asked if I remembered him and all the rest of it. He looked rather nice, and we were getting on famously when suddenly he said, 'Oh – there's a crowd of fellows who want to be introduced!' And with that, I was suddenly surrounded by undergraduates – about half a dozen of them, Michael Barnsley told me their names – I don't remember one of them! and they all told me how good I was and said they were going to be in the front row next time.

I simply stood there – too flabbergasted to know what to do. I was presented with a large box of chocolates, told it was from all of them, and at last, in sheer desperation, I caught Mr Colegrove, the business manager's eye, and he understood, and came and sent them away very nicely. They all said goodbye – not in the least abashed and left me standing there with the chocolates.

I knew that Claud Gurney had seen what was happening, so I went to his room and said, 'Mr Gurney, what am I to do?'

I told him about the chocolates and the young man who wanted to take me out to tea, and asked him if I ought to go, and if I should take these things. He was fearfully nice to me then, and said, 'Get all you can out of them – it's quite all right for you to take the chocolates or flowers or anything else they like to give you – you've earned those things. Go out to lunch and tea with your young men, that's quite all right, but for Heaven's sake don't fall in love with any of them.'

I assured him that I had no intention of doing so, that the one thing I was interested in was acting, and we had a long talk about that.

It was a short season with the Oxford Players, but a very worthwhile one. But a year or so later my mother was walking along in the West End with her sister Moira when she suddenly said, 'Quick, we must hide in this doorway!'

'Why?' asked Moira.

As they hid in the doorway Claud Gurney passed by.

'Why didn't you say hello?' asked Moira.

'I couldn't. I haven't got a job at the moment, and he might think I was pestering him for work.'

What a hopeless attitude! A perfect opportunity presented itself to meet him quite naturally, and she avoided it.

She observes that nowadays students are told that, without being unpleasant, they have to find a way of making people take notice. One actress she remembers in particular, Patience Collier, had the right idea and left no stone unturned. She was fearless, because she knew how talented she was. Patricia once asked her, in amazement at her audacity, 'Don't producers get fed up with you telephoning them every week?'

Patience explained that when she was working at Broadcasting House she would ring them and say, 'I'm just letting you know that I'm in the building and taking advantage of a free phone-call. I'm working this week, but free the next.'

One irritated BBC producer asked Patricia, 'Do you know an actress called Patience Collier? She writes to me every single week, and sends press notices. I'm never going to employ her.'

Three weeks later someone else in the same department had given her a job.

The truth is that, as an actor, you have to be part commercial traveller. My mother says that she can sell almost anything she believes in, except herself! Unfortunately your own attitude affects people's feelings towards you, if you lack confidence in yourself so will others.

My mother used to feel that she tended to get parts that other people could not, or would not, do. It did come as rather a surprise years later when it happened with her own 12-year-old son!

Howard Rose, a well-known BBC radio producer, was in the process of casting his new production of Shakespeare's *King John*. 'I'd like to get Patricia Hayes' son, Richard, to play Prince Arthur. If, because of school, he is not available, I suppose we'll have to have Pat!'

It is very easy to become type-cast as an actor. My mother always fought it, and has been fortunate in being able to be versatile, but it has been a struggle. When 'Coronation Street' was being cast originally she was approached, but she was not available at the time. Had she been free she would probably have gone into 'Coronation Street' – and might still be in it now. She would have made a lot of money, but could not have developed her acting talent in the ways she has been able to by being cast in such a variety of parts.

Fortune, too, plays a large part in all our lives, but absolutely rules actors' careers, especially in the early stages.

An anecdote that illustrates this is one told to my mother by a producer who was called in to produce 'Coronation Street', and thought he would do some initial pruning – planning to cut out a few characters and introduce some new ones. He started his project, ending one established artist's contract. As fate would have it, this producer was only with the series for a few weeks. After he had moved on he felt that he had done something rather contemptible; one poor soul who had felt secure in a job would never know why she was suddenly whisked out of the programme for no really valid reason (such as a poor performance), and no further changes were made.

After the Oxford Players there was another long period out of work. In desperation, Florence went to see Kenneth Barnes at RADA about Patricia's plight.

'Mr Barnes, why is Patricia out of work? Surely the fact that she won the Gold Medal should guarantee her career?'

'Don't worry, Mrs Hayes. Patricia's turn will come,' he reassured her as he showed her the door.

One day my mother read in *The Stage* – the actors' newspaper – that a nightclub in Leicester Square was having a competition night for 'turns', and auditions were being held all through that day.

'So I went up there armed with a piece of music; there was a pianist there, and I did my impersonation of Gracie Fields. They said, "Right – come along tonight, dear – get here at about 11 p.m." My mother came with me because I was a little apprehensive; I had never been to a nightclub before.

'We arrived at this place and they said, "Yes – go through along there, dear, go down the stairs; you will find a dressing-room there." The club was already full, and the cabaret (which was what this competition night was going to be) was due to start shortly. I was told to get ready and they would call me when they needed me. We sat in the dressing-room, and the time went by, and they still did not call me. It was a small room, and there was no sign of any ladies' cloakroom – or men's, for that matter. My mother opened the door and asked if there was a ladies' room. "Sorry, madam – no." There were waiters walking by with trays, and my mother asked another one, "Is there any sort of a cloak-room?" "No, madam – sorry." After a while I said to my mother, "I am desperate to go; I won't be able to sing my song unless I can spend a penny first." "I don't know what we can do," she said. "Ask the next person who passes by if they can bring us a cup," I suggested desperately. So my mother went out and I heard her mumbling in the corridor, then we heard voices shouting, one after another, "A lady would like a cup!" "A lady would like a cup!" It faded away into the distance as this piece of information was passed along the corridor from one waiter to another. Eventually there was a knock at the door and a cup was handed in. I had to use it but it really wasn't adequate.'

Nothing is remembered about the competition itself!

A short time later Patricia was sent to see Jevon Brandon Thomas, who ran a yearly Brandon Thomas Season that toured some of the major cities and summer resorts.

Jevon was the son of Walter Brandon Thomas who wrote *Charley's Aunt*, the brilliant comedy that was an enormous hit when it was first written in 1892 and is still performed regularly to this day. There was a certain amount of family money, which had enabled Jevon to set up his project. He had the idea of running a stock company, choosing six plays with interchangeable scenery. He would then assemble a cast of able actors of varying ages and once the plays were rehearsed they would commence the tour. They tended to play a few weeks in each venue rather than moving every week. Jevon had two sisters, Amy and Sylvia. Sylvia wanted to be a ballerina and in the early days Jevon would always start the evening with a ballet Prologue, performed by Sylvia and a male dancer.

Patricia, now twenty-one, was hired as an *ingénue*. She vividly remembers thinking that the other actors were absolutely marvellous. However, when her mother came to see the shows her views were not quite so enthusiastic.

'What do you think of So-and-So?' asked Patricia.

'Quite good.'

'*Quite good*! He is marvellous!'

'He is a bit amateurish.'

'Well – do you like our leading lady?'

'Unfortunately, she has a very annoying habit of nodding her head on every single line.'

My mother had not noticed these things, but realized afterwards that they were absolutely true. It was not only the other actors who attracted Florence's criticism; she was always Patricia's sternest critic, but an invaluable asset. Harsh, truthful and invariably accurate.

'You are getting into bad habits.'

'Am I?'

'Yes – you keep on fidgeting, shifting about.'

'I'm meant to – it's a fidgety sort of part.'

'Is that what Jevon told you?'

'Yes – he said that she's a very fidgety sort of girl.' (She invented that.)

As soon as her mother had left, Patricia took a closer look at her performance and noticed that she was indeed fidgeting on stage. She remedied it immediately.

During June 1931, the company was in Birmingham and one of the actresses, Rita Brunstrom, asked Jevon if she could go down to London during the week. He refused her permission, quite rightly, on the grounds that she might not be back in time for the performance. She decided that she would risk it and go anyhow, hoping that Jevon would not discover that she had gone. Unfortunately for her, someone told him of her intention. The play to be performed that night was Noël Coward's *Home Chat*.

When Jevon realized what was happening, he summoned Patricia and said, 'I want you to learn the part of Janet Ebony' (Rita Brunstrom's part) 'and if she goes to London, you will go on – whether she is back or not.'

Patricia had one night and a day to learn the part. A student staying in the same lodgings, who was rather keen on her, sat up all night and helped her learn the lines. The role was that of a more mature character than she usually played; but to everyone's amazement it was not only a competent performance that Patricia gave, but an inspired one. The press and the public were led to believe that Rita Brunstrom was sick. The *Birmingham Evening Despatch* said:

YOUNG ACTRESS'S TRIUMPH
Great Achievement by Patricia Hayes

No one who saw Noël Coward's *Home Chat* last night would have imagined that its leading lady, eight hours previously, had no idea that she would be playing the part – had, in fact, never seen the play.

Yet it was so. Rita Brunstrom, who had been cast for the part, fell ill; so did her understudy, and the producers were 'up against it', until Patricia Hayes gallantly stepped into the breach and offered to take the role.

She made herself word-perfect, and carried off a very unconventional role with flying colours, so that at the end she had to take quite a number of 'curtains' from a very enthusiastic house.

The *Birmingham Daily Mail* critic wrote:

Miss Hayes gave a fluent and confident rendering, full of the little artistic touches which many an actress of greater experience would be content to add after long rehearsal.

The *Birmingham Gazette* splashed:

ACTRESS'S TRIUMPH IN BIRMINGHAM
Star Part Learned in Eight Hours

A star arose in the theatrical sky last night. The Brandon Thomas Company, at The Theatre Royal, has been giving the best of modern dramas during the last few weeks – change of programme twice weekly.

Last night, Rita Brunstrom was billed as the star of Noël Coward's play *Home Chat*.

Miss Brunstrom fell ill. She had no understudy, and at 11 o'clock yesterday morning the cry arose at rehearsal, 'Who'll do the part?'

When Miss Patricia Hayes said, 'I'll take Miss Brunstrom's part,' the management was very relieved.

Miss Hayes had not even seen *Home Chat*, but between 11 o'clock yesterday morning and the raising of the curtain at 7.30, she learned the part and she acted it with distinction.

It was wonderful. Miss Hayes is not only the possessor of a good memory. She is an artist.

From this time onwards Jevon's concept of my mother completely changed and he began to cast her in much more challenging and interesting roles and subsequently re-engaged her for a second season as one of his leading ladies.

4

West End & Stratford Debuts

During her second season with Jevon a tall, handsome young man was engaged as a juvenile; his name – James Mason. He had just come down from Cambridge, had not been to Drama School and was a complete beginner. Apparently he was stiff and awkward on stage but had great intelligence and determination, and applied these qualities to his acting with the dedication and single-mindedness that make for rapid growth.

My mother is a very generous actress. Her portrayal of any character always includes those on stage with her, and the aura that she creates inspires the inexperienced to greater heights than their capability would normally allow. James Mason quickly became aware of this quality.

'Mrs Hayes, I love acting with your daughter.'

'Oh, do you, James? I wonder why that is?'

'It is because when I'm acting with her, I feel as if I'm a good actor. Unfortunately, when I'm not acting with her, I realize that I am not!'

Another young actor to join Jevon during that second season was the late Leonard Sachs; my mother and he became, and always remained, wonderful platonic friends. At that time, as an actress, she had a great deal to impart to Leonard, but he had far more flair and sense of style than she had, so that he would advise her on what to wear for auditions and interviews, knowing that so much casting was done on appearance first and foremost. He even managed to have her costumes for the season remodelled to suit the more petite figure. There is nothing worse than having to make-do with a costume that was originally made for a much larger woman! Feeling and looking right are extremely important on stage.

She, James Mason and Leonard Sachs became a threesome and had tremendous fun together in their formative years. James Mason, in his autobiography *Before I Forget*, remembered the times they shared with great affection, while Leonard Sachs says, 'She, James and I did everything together. We worked very hard indeed and yet managed to have a lot of fun. I can remember rolling down a hillside with your mother whilst on an after-lunch walk with a fan of ours.

'James was sort of in love with Patricia. He was not a very good actor then – but he became one. When he came to us, I put his first make-up on. We became very great friends. He and I used to smoke a cheap brand of cigarettes during the week, and on Fridays – payday – we bought a more expensive one.'

Leonard was very impressed with my mother's acting ability and stressed that her dramatic range was fantastic. When she played the waif, Tessa, in *The Constant Nymph*, a play adapted by Basil Dean from Margaret Kennedy's novel, she used to make him cry every night.

Alternatively, she played a Peruvian vamp very convincingly in a comedy by C.K. Munro called *At Mrs Beam's*. This play featured a group of lodgers in a London boardinghouse. The *Bournemouth Times and Directory* reported:

> Charming and winsome, Patricia Hayes is quite a startling surprise as the fiery little Laura Pasquale, who thinks nothing of throwing knives at her lover, and breaks out in a torrent of invective which completely floors the voluble busybody, Miss Shoe.

Leonard was playing an innocent, a nervously enamoured young man called Colin. During one of the performances, as the curtain went up, my mother was to be seen lying across his lap on the settee, in the process of seducing him, when she completely forgot her lines. Under her breath she whispered, 'What do I say?'. Leonard, thinking quickly, gazed down at her and whispered ardently (as a prompt), 'Kiss me, Colin!' From then on they were always in grave danger of collapsing in a heap of laughter during the scene.

In complete contrast to both of these roles she also played Mary Rose in J.M. Barrie's masterpiece of the same name. It is interesting to note that the play was written at the request of one of Sir James Barrie's godsons, who asked him to write something 'creepy'. It certainly *is* creepy. Once again the press had rich praise for my mother's interpretation of the part. The *Eastbourne Chronicle* stated:

> We have waited for an opportunity to see Miss Patricia Hayes in a part worthy of her skill, and in the title role of *Mary Rose* the hope is realized. Miss Hayes completely sinks her personality into that of Barrie's heroine, and so thoroughly does she do it that no member of the audience can regard her as other than Mary Rose, the delicate little lady who answers the call of the mysterious island in the Outer Hebrides. There is a charm and conviction in her portrayal of the character that compels the deepest admiration.

Jevon, thrilled at her versatility, had started to cast her in the widest variety of parts.

She was with Jevon for three of his tours, and could have stayed with him indefinitely, but began to get restless, feeling that she was not progressing. The shortcomings of some of her fellow actors had become obvious to her, and she wanted to change her own style, so she went to Jevon and said, 'I'd like to try and get work in London now.'

'Fine – do that – there's nothing good enough for you in the next two or three plays. Give London a go. I'll always fit you in again if you want to come back.'

So off she went to the big city. As usual it was a long time before anything cropped up, but eventually someone wanted to come out of a play and she got her chance.

The play was *Children in Uniform* by Christa Winslow. The action takes place in Germany, and tells the story of a young girl, Manuela, who is orphaned and is sent to boarding-school. She is at the delicate emotional age of puberty and develops an enormous crush on one of the mistresses – Fräulein von Bernberg, who is very kind to her and has an enormously charismatic personality.

As part of a special school feast the girls put on a little play. During the party afterwards, they are allowed cider to drink and Manuela gets a little tipsy. She jumps on a table and shouts the praises of the 'wonderful Fräulein von Bernberg!', and then collapses.

The other mistresses who have witnessed this exhibition report her, and as a punishment for this absolutely shocking behaviour she is put into solitary confinement. No one may speak to her. While she is isolated in this way, the Grand Duchess comes to visit the school and, because she knew Manuela's parents, Manuela is presented to her. The Grand Duchess shakes her hand and comments that she knew her mother and father very well and what wonderful people they were.

The memory of her tragic loss and the loneliness of her solitary confinement prove too much for Manuela, who goes to the top of the grand staircase and throws herself to her death.

Having heard this dramatic story, it may be surprising to hear that Patricia did not get the part of Manuela. Jessica Tandy played it and, according to my mother, was marvellous. However, a girl who was playing one of the smaller parts – we'll call her Jenny – was left a fortune by a relative in India, and was advised to go to India to oversee the settlement of the estate herself. This created a vacancy, and, having heard about it, my mother lost no time in going to see the company manager, Barbara Nixon, and asking for the role. Barbara Nixon said, 'Yes – you will be fine to take over. Come and see Jenny a few times. Then you'll have two weeks' rehearsals and you can take over the part.'

A one-year-old Patricia with her wonderful nurse, Sister Reeve.

In the Banstead countryside, Patricia (standing) and her sister Moira play with a friend.

Mrs Hayes and her brood (*left to right*) Brian, Moira and Patricia.

In playful mood, Patricia (aged five) enjoying the sun.

Patricia in a fairy costume for one of her very first roles. Note the warm vest!

Moira and Patricia posing in best frocks, made by Mother.

Patricia discussing her winning entry for the *Daily Mail* sandbuilding competition with the judges. Ramsgate, circa 1920.

Patricia with a companion from *Circus Boy,* a play by Michael Redgrave,
Liverpool, 1935.

The play had originally been cast and rehearsed by a formidable German woman director called Leontine Sagan, who had also directed the very successful film of the same title. My mother had auditioned with all the hundreds of young hopefuls, but never even got through the first round!

Jenny's part was tiny but showy – she had one short scene in which all the attention was directed on her. My mother admits that she was not brilliant when she first took over, but gradually made the part her own and became extremely good in it, getting laughs for her little dance.

She was considerably older than most of the girls in the dressing-room, who were very young. At first they were not very friendly towards her but they grew warmer – especially when they discovered that she was good at reading character from handwriting! They were intrigued and would bring in letters from their boyfriends to find out more about them, or put Patricia to the test by showing her samples of their fathers' handwriting.

'What's he like? This will show if you can really do it.'

'Well, he's extremely neat and orderly, and good at gardening.'

'How did you know that he was good at gardening?'

'This is the handwriting of a good gardener.'

There was no further explanation; but she was invariably right.

Six months after she took over in *Children in Uniform*, Jevon Brandon Thomas contacted her. 'I've taken the Wimbledon Theatre and the King's Theatre, Hammersmith, for a season of my stock theatre. The play I shall open with is *Old Heidelberg*, and I'd like you to play the lead.'

She had played it already on one of his tours. After due consideration she decided she wanted to do Jevon's season, and was going to give two weeks' notice when he was ready, as you could in those days.

At around the same time, Jenny, the original girl from *Children in Uniform*, returned from India and began hanging around the theatre. One day the company manager called my mother in to see her and said, 'I want to warn you, because I don't want you to get a terrible shock, but when you leave the theatre on Friday they are going to hand you your notice. Jenny has asked for her part back, and the powers-that-be have agreed to let her have it back. Don't be upset.'

'Well, as a matter of fact, I was going to hand in my notice in a month's time anyhow because I've got another job to go to,' said my mother.

Jenny had wheedled her way back in with the management in a rather sly way. When the other girls in the dressing-room discovered what had happened they were absolutely furious. They thought it was a despicable thing to do when someone else had taken over a part. It's a good thing my mother did not have a chance to interpret Jenny's handwriting; who knows what she might have read into it!

Patricia duly received her notice to leave *Children in Uniform* and two weeks later commenced rehearsals for Jevon as Heidi in *Old Heidelberg*.

Old Heidelberg had great sentimental value for Jevon Brandon Thomas, for it had been written by R. Bleichmann, a good friend of his fathers. Some years later it was re-written, set to music and called *The Student Prince*. However, Jevon's production did not immediately make money and his backers let him down, so he hurriedly cancelled the rest of the season and the whole project fell through. He had planned to make this a stepping-stone into West End management, but the catastrophe, as he saw it, ended his ambitions, and it was his last venture. Who knows what golden opportunities might have opened up for my mother had he succeeded?

When my mother was in London, she and her friends used to spend many hours at the Interval Club in Soho. It sounds quite spicy doesn't it? A club in Soho! On the contrary, it was nicknamed 'an oasis of innocence in a desert of vice'.

During the 1930s the Catholic Stage Guild saw the need for a club for Catholic actors and actresses. It was finally started by a most remarkable woman, Mrs Balvaird Hewett, and run by her and her formidable and extremely difficult daughter Molly. They inevitably fell out with the Catholic Stage Guild almost straight away, because the committee annoyed them, but they continued to run the Club as a private concern.

The Interval Club performed a valuable service for both actors and writers. If you were rehearsing or performing and there was a long period of the day when there was nowhere to go, you could pop into the Club for a meal or a chat with your colleagues. The food there was extremely good, really delicious plain home-cooking, and inexpensive. A few people lived there permanently. The Hewetts even took a further annex around the corner to accommodate others.

The address was 22 Dean Street. It was an unprepossessing edifice in need of a coat of paint, but the door was open to rich and poor actors alike. A narrow staircase led to the first floor, which consisted mainly of one long room with a very basic stage and a consistently out-of-tune piano. This room was leased out to theatres and film companies for rehearsals and provided some necessary income, because the Club's membership fees were nominal.

Most of the actors who frequented the Club were permanently unemployed; in fact my mother used to get very annoyed with other actors who fled when they became successful. Bernard Lee explained, 'I can't go back there when I am doing so well and see all those poor people who never get any work.'

'But you should go back! When they see that you have had success, it gives them heart,' reprimanded my mother.

Among the motley crowd of would-be actors there were some unforgettable personalities such as Eugene Leahy, an ageing and usually bad-tempered old Irish actor with a heart of gold, who was very deaf. The Christmas festivities were magnificent, and as children we often went there for the Christmas Day party. There would be a brightly lit tree, a nativity play, frequently written by Moira and produced by Patricia, a huge traditional Christmas dinner and, somewhere in the lounge-room, a crib with all the figures rather roughly hewn from wood by Eugene Leahy.

One particular Christmas this good Catholic man was making the crib; he must have miscalculated the size of the figures and, as he tried to force St Joseph into the stable, he was heard to say in a very loud voice, such as only the newly deaf can summon, 'Get in there, you bloody Jew!'

Molly Hewett was another great character. She also had a heart of gold, but she and her mother made the rules of the Club, and Molly enforced them in an uncompromising fashion. There used to be a menu, and on Fridays the main course would be fish (those were the days when it was a mortal sin for a Catholic to eat meat on Fridays), but for the non-Catholics there would be a meat alternative.

One day a woman came in and ordered the steak and kidney pie, and Molly said accusingly, 'It is Friday, you know.'

'I'll still have the steak and kidney.'

'You can't – you are a Catholic.'

'I'm ordering the steak and kidney pie, Molly!'

From then on Molly never served a meat dish on Fridays. I wonder if she was protecting the eternal souls of the Catholic members, or if she was annoyed at being thwarted.

My mother once had a mammoth row with Molly, and finally said, 'That's it! I'm leaving!'

Mrs Balvaird Hewett saw my mother putting on her hat and coat, and asked where she was going.

'I can't stand Molly a moment longer. She is so unfair and unpleasant. I'm leaving – and I'm not coming back!'

'Come here, Patricia – don't cut off your nose to spite your face. Don't think to yourself that because you are in the right, and you probably are, that it is a good reason to leave the Club. You are one of the few people who can stand up to Molly, and you should say to yourself I'm staying on here and if Molly does anything that I disapprove of then I'll stand up to her.' So Patricia went away and decided that Molly's mother was right.

Molly absolutely adored her mother; when she died all

Molly wanted to do was be with her mother again. 'I have work to do here,' she said, 'and I shall carry on and do it, but I cannot wait to be with my mother again.' Great faith like this is truly enviable.

The Interval Club is a sad loss; perhaps it would still be going today if all the rehearsal rooms didn't have their own canteens and relaxation areas. In the BBC every building has its own restaurant; many theatres nowadays have canteens with subsidized food. Molly was very upset when the final lease ended and it was decided to close the Club; but she realized that it was no longer needed and so an era ended.

James Mason and Leonard Sachs were among the friends who frequented the Interval Club with my mother. Leonard Sachs mentions that James Mason was 'sort of in love with Patricia' on the tour with Jevon. The fact is that James had fallen in love with my mother and remained so for a long time. He once confided to a mutual friend, as he was about to return to London after a season in Dublin, 'I'm going back to London – and I'm going to marry Patricia.'

My mother, on the other hand, although very fond of James, was not ready for a relationship, but they remained very good friends. They did not always see eye to eye, and it used to annoy her when he deliberated a long time over his principles during an argument. She has always been impatient of people who are slow to answer. Apparently he wrote her the most marvellous letters; he could take as long as he liked over those! I wonder where they are?

James came to the Interval Club one day, and approached my mother who was sitting with a group of her friends. He leant over and whispered confidentially, 'I was wondering if you would like to have tea with me today?'

'Oh, yes, that would be lovely.'

'Well – shall we have it here, or would you like to come round to my flat and have it there?'

'Let's have it here!'

Poor James, he must have kicked himself for giving her the option.

Nevertheless, he soon moved into the world of stardom and later he married and spent most of his life in America. Patricia lost touch with him, although she once had a very small role in a film in which he was starring. Being inexperienced in film work, she asked him for some advice. 'You have no need to worry about overacting, because you always hit the nail on the head,' he told her. 'However, technically, an actor must remember not to use his mouth too much, it looks ugly on the big screen. Use your eyes as much as you like but use the lower part of your face as little as possible in film-work.'

In 1934 Patricia auditioned for the Royal Shakespeare Company and Bridges Adams, who was in control, offered her Ariel in *The Tempest*, and the part of the boy in *Henry V*. She was thrilled about Ariel – ever since her sister had flown in *The Bluebird* she had longed to fly, and that year Ariel was to fly.

Just before rehearsals were due to commence my mother was taken ill with appendicitis, followed by peritonitis. The Royal Shakespeare Company would not let her fly without a medical report confirming that she was well enough to do so but the doctors said that it would not be safe so soon after the operation. She lost the part of Ariel, which was given to Rachel Kempson, who was already playing Juliet in *Romeo and Juliet*. This was a great disappointment to my mother, though she did play Moth in *Love's Labours Lost* as well as the boy in *Henry V*. She had some excellent reviews.

> Little Miss Patricia Hayes gave one of the best performances ever seen in Stratford as the boy [in *Henry V*] who follows the dubious fortunes of Pistol, Nym and Bardolph. If Festival medals were given, Miss Hayes would deserve an added bar.
> *Birmingham Mail*

> After Mr John Wyse, the best performance was by the youngest member of the company, Miss Patricia Hayes, who played the boy unnamed, servant to that remarkable trio,

Pistol, Nym and Bardolph. She has one of the most difficult tasks, which is to hold the stage by herself and speak direct to the audience. She does so, and that, indeed, is the whole secret of Shakespearean acting.

Birmingham Post

Patricia Hayes as Moth, the page [in *Love's Labours Lost*] was in her degree the best thing in the play.

Daily Telegraph

For the second time in the week, Miss Patricia Hayes distinguished herself as a boy, and her Moth was a delightful pendant to the production.

The Times

She had had some of the best reviews of the season, but it was to be forty years before she was asked to go back to Stratford again!

The following Christmas, my mother was asked if she would like to join the Liverpool Repertory Company to be in a Christmas play to be written and directed by the young Michael Redgrave. He was already married to Rachel Kempson, with whom my mother had worked at Stratford. The play was called *Circus Boy* and she was given the lead, Ludo. She describes it as a very strenuous part. Rachel Kempson had suggested her for this, after seeing her playing boys so successfully at Stratford. Although a play for children, it was extremely well written, and she enjoyed renewing her friendship with Rachel.

During the short season she also met, and became very friendly with, a young actress called Penelope Dudley-Ward, whose mother was a great socialite. Penelope's father had been almost perpetually away, either on safari in Africa or on some extended expedition to far-flung parts of the world. Eventually her mother had divorced him, and become a great friend and the constant companion of the Prince of Wales.

According to Penelope, in all the years that her mother was with David (the family name for the Prince of Wales) he

relied on her to make most of the decisions regarding the
content of his speeches, or about what to wear at the many
functions that he had to attend. He was also extremely
helpful to Mrs Dudley-Ward with the charity work that was
her passion, and he adored Penelope and her sister Angela:
they called him Uncle David. Eventually, Mrs Dudley-Ward
ended the relationship because she wanted to be in a position
to remarry, but they remained good friends and he still
continued to ask her advice even when he had other women
friends. However, according to Penelope, as soon as he met
Mrs Simpson, he had nothing more to do with any of them,
even to the extent of cutting them dead in public.

Later, back in London, Penelope invited my mother to
stay at the family mansion for a week while the rest of her
family were away. It was an amazing experience. The two of
them were waited on hand and foot by numerous servants.
Then Penelope was called away, suddenly and unexpectedly,
but she insisted that my mother stay on for the rest of the
week.

'I can't stay here on my own with all the servants.'

'Yes, you can. I have told the servants you will be staying.'

So she stayed, but she found it really hard to become
accustomed to the attention.

'What would you like for dinner, Miss Hayes?'

'Just something light. Don't go to any trouble.'

'It is no trouble, Miss Hayes. Might I suggest the smoked
trout, followed by a little pheasant?'

'Thank you, that will be fine.'

My mother returned home to reality at the end of the
week. No servants, no mansion – and no work.

5

A West End Success
& Wedding Bells

During the year 1935 Leonard Sachs and his great friend, Peter Ridgeway, decided to put some shows together. Initially they put on some Sunday plays. These were an important part of the theatrical scene at the time. Anyone who had a play that seemed worth while could try it out with the minimum of expense. Actors gave their services free of charge, in the hope that the play would be seen by financial backers and transfer to the West End.

Eventually Peter and Leonard came up with the idea of starting a club for actors and other night-birds to visit after the normal theatres had closed. Somewhere to relax after a show, have a drink and a meal, and watch some light and amusing entertainment.

The most important object was to find a venue for their project, and finally they went to have a look at a place in Covent Garden. It had been turned into a little theatre by Dorita Curtis-Heywood but it was not a success. By the time Leonard and Peter saw it, it had degenerated into a rather seedy nightclub. Undaunted by this, or by the fact that they only had 2s 6d between them, they bought the remains of the lease from the owner.

They then set about gathering material for their first show.

They decided that it was to be a genuine Old Time Music Hall, a series of songs and scenas presented in authentic Victorian style. Harold Scott, an authority on Victorian music hall, researched all the musical numbers. He was a fine musician and discovered some very original songs, such as 'I'd choose to be a daisy' and ''Tis I vow and swear'.

Leonard and Peter circularized the London Theatres, inviting all the actors to *The Late Joys* at 'Evans Song and Supper Room', for an entertainment after their own shows had finished. (My mother was in these very first shows, dressed as a choirboy, with three other actresses, up in a little gallery, singing 'I'd choose to be a daisy'.) The show caught on immediately, and at the end of three weeks it was a sensational success. Everyone in the theatre world was talking about it, and all the stars of the day were to be seen there, supping and watching the highly polished Victorian entertainment. This was the very beginning of the Players Theatre, which is now situated underneath the railway arches at Charing Cross, and still carries on all the old traditions established in those very early days.

Leonard and Peter knew that they must keep going and strike while the iron was hot. Harold Scott, their previous collaborator, was not available for a while so they replaced him, which was a shame, since he had been one of the originals, but with such a success on their hands they had to continue. Unfortunately, Peter Ridgeway died in the first year; and Leonard, who had never really wanted to run the theatre himself, was left holding the baby. 'I just wanted to be a famous actor, go to Hollywood and have a swimming pool!' he says.

Leonard was always the chairman. He wanted my mother to sing a solo, but she was very unsure of her ability. They decided that she would appear as a boy and sing 'Kiss me, Mother, ere I die', a war song about a boy who is off to fight in the Boer War. They put her in a Victorian sailor suit with a cotton sailor collar and a round wide-awake sailor hat. Leonard introduced her as: 'That miracle of mellifluousness, my own son – Master Pat Hayes.'

She was very nervous to begin with, and would laugh when the audience laughed, and forget her words or the tune. They cleverly managed to incorporate that into the performance; if she went wrong, she would hang her head down and walk off and Leonard would make excuses for his son. 'Ladies and gentleman, he is very young! Please make allowances.'

The audiences adored it. Soon afterwards a song called 'Put me in my little bed' was rehearsed, and it became another winner. She gradually gained confidence, and became absolutely brilliant. Her admirers would come to watch her night after night.

The Players Theatre turned out to be a magnificent stable out of which emerged some of the most famous English stage personalities – Alec Clunes, Robert Edison, Bernard Miles, Peter Ustinov, Vida Hope, and many more. Other people became so adept at performing the Victorian songs that they were quite happy to remain at the Players Theatre most of their working lives. The great Joan Sterndale-Bennett and the unique Archie Harradine are examples of this. They had special songs which only they would perform, which people would love to see them repeat over and over again. It is interesting to note that, though Archie Harradine had one of the worst stutters imaginable off stage, he was notable for his brilliant and devastatingly fast patter songs. My mother was able to perform at the Players whenever she did not have other employment, which was a great way of keeping herself in practice and in the public eye.

She was at the Interval Club one day when she received a message that playwright/actor Emlyn Williams (who she had recently worked with in a Sunday play) and actor/producer Miles Malleson wanted her to go to the Duchess Theatre to audition for Emlyn Williams' new play, *Night Must Fall*. A friend at the club asked her what she intended to wear, and offered to lend her her fur coat. All her friends helped to get her ready for this important interview, and shortly afterwards she set off, in the borrowed fur and some crippling high heels, to walk from Dean Street to the Duchess Theatre. The doorman at the stage-door told her to go upstairs to the next floor, and the first person she came face to face with was Emlyn Williams – who said, 'Hullo, Patricia. Has somebody lent you a fur coat?'

Miles Malleson interviewed her, but it was Emlyn Williams himself who had suggested her for one of the roles. She did not get the part, being told that she looked too young. However, she was offered the understudy; and rather than be out of work she took that. Betty Jardine, whose part she was covering, said, 'Oh, I am sorry for you, because I am never off. I am the sort of person who manages to drag themselves on no matter how appalling I feel. I think I would go on if I was dying.'

But the day did come when my mother got a message telling her she was 'on' that night. Betty Jardine had tonsilitis, and the doctors thought she would be off for at least a week. My mother learnt the lesson that all understudies have to learn. Everyone is absolutely thrilled with you when you go on at short notice; but from then on the other actors spend their time trying to make you give exactly the same performance as the indisposed person's.

'Please say your line a little quicker.'

'Betty used to do this – or that – or whatever.'

'Betty always used to stand facing me during that line, so that the audience can see my expression.'

Finally you end up trying to copy the other person. Then comes the bitter moment when you hear other actors saying, 'Oh, Betty, thank God you are back.' They do not mean to hurt, but it is very painful.

She vowed there and then that she would never understudy again, and luckily she never had to.

Emlyn Williams was asked to take *Night Must Fall* to America with the full English cast; but as the play was still a hit in the West End, a new London cast was auditioned. This time my mother was offered the role she had been understudying. She did not hesitate in accepting, and she opened at the Cambridge Theatre on 10 July 1936.

'Miss Patricia Hayes's maidservant is a little gem of a

performance', said the *News Chronicle*.

One afternoon, my mother looked up from her chair in the lounge-room at the Interval Club to see a rather attractive young man coming in. She watched him out of the corner of her eye as he hung his hat on the hat-stand and sat down quietly with his newspaper. She wasted no time in getting to know him. He was an actor/author, later to become very famous, called Gerald Savory. They instantly took a liking to one another, the main reason being that they made each other laugh so much. He was an extremely witty person and my mother has a unique sense of the ridiculous.

Shortly afterwards he began to pick her up from the Cambridge Theatre every night, after *Night Must Fall*, and to see her to Waterloo Station, where she would catch the train home to Wimbledon. On their way to the station they would often stop for a cup of tea or coffee. One night they were having tea together in a darkened tea-room when she remarked, 'Gerald, you are terribly sentimental and I'm not. Sentimental people put me off!'

'Do you really think I'm sentimental? In what way?' he asked.

'Well – you are the kind of person who would kiss a lump of sugar before popping it into my tea.'

Whereupon he picked up a lump of sugar, kissed it, popped it into her tea-cup, and passed it to her. This he proceeded to do for ever after.

Another night on that well-trodden path to Waterloo, Gerald remembers quite clearly that he was trying to talk my mother into joining Actors' Equity, the actors' union which had just been started. She was very against any form of union for actors, feeling that it was out of place in an artistic field where talent should be the overriding factor. As they were crossing Waterloo Bridge, in desperation he said, 'If you will join Equity, I will throw my hat in the river.'

'OK, then – I will join!'

Away went the hat, last seen heading towards Westminster

on a rising tide.

Their 'relationship' lasted a long time and they probably got through a number of hats and a great many lumps of sugar. When questioned about exactly what kind of 'relationship' it was, my mother says, 'We were keen on each other.'

Gerald Savory, on the other hand, says, 'I was madly in love with her, and almost thought I was engaged to her until I went to Hull as an actor and she took up with someone else.'

Inevitably, actors have to go on tour; and at a time when Gerald was away Bernard Lee began frequenting the Interval Club. He was involved with a lady but, despite this, my mother fell hopelessly in love with him. She lost no time in writing to Gerald, telling him that it was all off because she had fallen madly in love with Bernard Lee, the actor. Some time later when she met Gerald he said, 'I got that letter from you in the morning. I went into the bathroom to shave and I propped it up on a little shelf in front of the mirror and started shaving. When I came to the bit about you falling in love with Bernard Lee and being unable to continue with me, I looked in the mirror and I had the razor in my hand. I thought, this is the moment when I should cut my throat. Then I thought, it's a bit messy. So I did not do it. Now I've got over you.'

How typical of human nature that, when he said he had got over her, she suddenly felt a great sense of disappointment. Fortunately, they remained very good friends and strangely enough he also got involved in a hopeless love affair. They must have been a great consolation to one another.

During a 'rest' period, Gerald began writing *George and Margaret*, the play that made him famous. He was living in Southampton Row with his mother, and Patricia used to pop round to see him. She always showed enormous interest in the play, and every time she went round a few more pages would have been written. He admits that, at that stage, she was the only person who showed any interest; she laughed a lot at it and gave him great encouragement. Finally, he came to the last scene, which must be every author's nightmare. How to end the play?

My mother made some suggestions and between them they concocted a marvellous finish. The play was an enormous success on the Sunday night trial and my mother played the juvenile lead; while Irene Handl played the character who brought the curtain and the house down! It was immediately taken up by H.M. Tennent Management, to be brought to the West End. Gerald Savory did not realize what a strong position he was in when it transferred; he could have insisted on having Patricia in the cast. But he was very young, and it was his first success. He came to her telling her, 'They are going to put on a West End production of my play, but they will not have you in it. I tried to insist, but they are determined to have a big name.'

My poor mother, what a disappointment it must have been! Gerald Savory thought that she took it very well, and was amazed that she was brave enough to go to the first night.

The play was an enormous success and he made a fortune. Half-jokingly, Patricia suggested to him that she should have a percentage, since she had inspired the ending. His reply was to offer her any gift she would like. Now comes a real insight into my mother. She could have had her own fur coat or some sparkling diamonds – anything. Instead, she asked for a brand-new Hoover vacuum cleaner. She had it for many years! It may even now be in her cellar, she is brilliant at repairing vacuum cleaners.

Eventually Gerald Savory went to America with *George and Margaret*; he subsequently married an American and remained there for many years. His personal life was full of tragedy. His first wife committed suicide. Later he married a woman who had two daughters from a previous marriage; he was extremely happy with this wife, and grew to adore the two girls. Suddenly his wife became extremely ill, and within three weeks she was dead. The children's real father then claimed his two daughters, and Gerald never saw them again.

He returned to England all alone, where he ultimately took up the post of Head of Drama for BBC Television. Now he is happily married to the actress Sheila Brennan.

It was at about this time that my mother met another young actress at the Interval Club, June Wenner. They got on very well from the moment they met and, as they both wanted to leave home, they decided to share a flat together. The apartment they rented consisted of two bedsits, a kitchen, bathroom and a spare room.

June and my mother shared many happy times at the flat for both were young, and relatively carefree, and they had their careers in common. They quickly learned how to cope with the day-to-day problems of living with another person. June was very fastidious and taught my mother many aspects of housekeeping that remain with her today.

They entertained their various boyfriends in what would seem the most respectable fashion today. One thing is certain, they laughed a lot over their problems and experiences. An anecdote illustrating the times they were living in involves one of their lodgers. They were quite hard up, and had decided to sublease the spare room to a friend, Mervyn, one of the most harmless and helpful of people. He was even prepared to move out for the weekend if they needed the space for a visiting relative.

One day June's mother came to stay for the weekend and, after she had had a long conversation with June, she took Patricia on one side. 'You will have to ask Mervyn to leave the flat. It is probably perfectly all right in London, but if any of our friends in the country discovered that June was sharing with a young man, they would never speak to us again.' So poor old Mervyn got the boot!

One evening Patricia's brother Brian came over to the flat and met June for the first time. From then onwards he was a very frequent visitor, and two years later they were married. I wonder what June's parents' neighbours felt about the fact that Brian was a Catholic?

Among the actors who frequent the Players Theatre was Valentine Rooke. (His real name was Valentine Cozens-Brooke, but he used Rooke as his professional name, it was less of a mouthful.) He was on the crest of an enormous professional success. He had left RADA in 1930, and gone straight to the West End. Absolutely brilliant in comedy, he had been heralded as one of the great hopes of the British Theatre by Patrick L. Mannock, the *Daily Herald*'s theatre critic, for his performance in *The Streets of London*. The Australian impresario, Sydney Carroll, then signed him up to appear in Wycherley's comedy, *The Country Wife*. After that he had performed numerous times in the Open Air Theatre in Regent's Park, working with such great actors and personalities as Bernard Shaw, Vivien Leigh, Lawrence Olivier and Flora Robson. However, Valentine was recovering from a broken love affair when he first met my mother, and he spent the first six months of his relationship with her getting it out of his system by talking of nothing else.

It appears that a few years earlier he had walked into a room where a crowd of students was playing table-tennis. Across the room he saw a girl (we'll call her Heidi) and *bang* – he fell madly in love with her.

Heidi was a young German, full of the utter selfishness that only youth and beauty can get away with. He pursued her relentlessly, and she did not really want him. He even went to Germany and met her family; but they were not pleasant to him, for they did not want their beautiful daughter to throw herself away on a young man who had chosen the most precarious of careers. Meanwhile, he had started asking her to marry him – but she always refused.

Heidi had a sister who lived in America, and she was always saying that if only she had the money she would love to go and visit her. Somehow Valentine managed to raise the money, and bought her a ticket to America, under the promise that she would not stay long. While Heidi was away, he had made for her, at Cartier's, the most beautiful gold bangle; it cost him a fortune. He sent it to her in America for her birthday and, true to form, she hardly acknowledged it. Time passed, and there was no sign of her return. Her reply to his query as to when she was coming back was that she could not afford the fare, so he borrowed the money and she returned. She had given the precious bangle to her sister, to thank her for letting her stay!

Valentine managed to persuade Heidi to live with him and, when she agreed, they moved into an apartment lent to them by a friend. He was always begging her to marry him and she always said no. One day he asked desperately, 'Heidi – why can't we get married?'

'All right, Valentine. You go and get the papers, make an appointment at the registry office, and I will marry you.'

Valentine told my mother, 'When she suddenly agreed, I was completely taken aback, but instead of being over the moon, my heart turned into a lump of lead and fell to the pit of my stomach!'

To prepare for their wedding, Heidi went back to Germany to 'sort out a few things'. Within two months she wrote to say that she was getting married to a man of her father's choice in Germany; her father had promised her a car if she would marry him. To add insult to injury, she invited Valentine to the wedding.

Valentine had always been able to memorize his lines with such facility that he was in the habit of reading a book in his dressing-room until the last minute, walking down the stairs still reading, and putting it down seconds before he was due to make an entrance. He was so upset by the loss of the woman around whom he had been building his entire life that his ability to concentrate abandoned him, and he forgot his lines so badly, on more than one occasion, that he lost all confidence on stage. When my mother met him, he was desperately trying to think of an alternative to acting. He also developed morbid fears of hurting people; these became known in the family as 'the nameless dreads'. One day he was with my mother when he had an attack and she made him tell her what it was. 'As I sit here talking to you, I am thinking how awful it would be if I suddenly took you by the throat and strangled you.'

My mother was not at all afraid, because she knew that he was not capable of any sort of violence; but she says that, strangely enough, she felt as if a devil had hopped out of him and entered her. The strain of the break-up and depression had unbalanced him for a while.

While June was getting to know Brian in her bedsit, Patricia was in hers, listening for hours on end to the way that Valentine had been treated and offering him sympathy and understanding. Human nature is so fickle that she was very attracted to him from the start; because he was a challenge, he held her interest, while others who were keen on her seemed to her so lacklustre.

One night J.B. Priestley came to the Players Theatre with Hazel Terry, and they watched my mother perform 'Put Me In My Little Bed'. Priestley thought she was marvellous, and said so to Hazel. 'This girl is a genius, but what else could she play?'

'Anything!' replied Hazel.

Shortly afterwards Patricia received a message at the Interval Club, asking her to attend the the first rehearsal of *When We Are Married*. She had been cast in the delightful role of Ruby Birtle.

Leonard Sachs says, 'At this stage Patricia did a very brave thing. The management of *When We Are Married* wanted to include a clause in her contract saying that she could not appear in any late-night performances at the Players Theatre during the run of the play. But Patricia said, "The Players Theatre are responsible for getting me this job, so if they want me during the run I shall do it!" ' Luckily, Priestley respected that, and the contract for her to play Ruby Birtle was signed.

When We Are Married is one of Priestley's masterpieces. Briefly, the story concerns three prosperous Yorkshiremen and their three self-satisfied wives, who are in the process of celebrating their joint silver wedding anniversary. During the evening they discover that the clergyman who married them was not fully ordained, and that they have seemingly been 'living in sin' for the last twenty-five years. All hell breaks loose, everybody cashing in on the sudden loss of dignity experienced by the self-important couples. Ruby Birtle is the cheeky little maid who enjoys the inevitable chaos.

The play was directed by Basil Dean, one of the top directors of the period. He had just gone into management with Priestley, mainly in the production of his plays. One of the first people to recognize the potential of 'talking' films as opposed to the 'silent movies', Basil Dean was a marvellous director with a wealth of experience. His autobiography, *Mind's Eye*, makes fascinating reading. In an article for the *Observer*, in 1938, he was asked to name six of England's best actors, chiefly with reference to comparatively new discoveries; his list consisted of: Flora Robson, Marjorie Fielding, Margaret Rutherford, Michael Redgrave, Patricia Hayes and Robert Edison.

However, Basil Dean had a reputation for being extremely demanding; and very harsh with his tongue. The story goes that he was working with a certain actor in another play, who was trying to come to grips with a rather difficult scene. Every time he asked for some assistance, Basil Dean would say, 'Use your imagination!' Again and again he repeated the phrase, until the exasperated actor burst out, 'Mr Dean, I am handing you an imaginary script. I am walking across this imaginary stage. I am going through this imaginary door – shutting the imaginary door behind me – and walking out of this imaginary theatre!' And out he went. It is probably not a true story, but it gives an idea of the kind of ordeal that Patricia was expecting. She was not disappointed.

It was customary in those days for actors to be put under a conditional contract for the first two weeks of the rehearsal period. If they did not come up to the director's expectations they would be given the sack and the part would be re-cast. It must have been with great excitement, and a certain amount of fear and trepidation, that she went off to those early rehearsals.

Ruby Birtle's first speech in *When We Are Married* consists of a long list of what her employers have on their menu for the celebration dinner that evening. Each time my mother came to rehearse that piece, she would see a look of exasperation coming over Basil Dean's face and he would shout, 'No – *no* – NO!' Can't you get it right? You are making too much of it.'

She felt that she was certain to get the sack, and the days crept nearer and nearer to the end of the fortnight. Suddenly, one morning, she had a breakthrough. Basil Dean shouted 'No – *no* – NO! You are giving me Kathleen Harrison, and what I want is Gracie Fields!'

The minute he said that, she realized exactly what he wanted. Her accent was right, but the spirit was wrong. She had always been a great fan of Gracie Fields, who had a wonderful off-hand manner, and this was what Dean had been after. Apparently, before her days at the Players Theatre, my mother had been famous for her imitation of Gracie Fields!

From then on the rehearsals went well, and she worked her way securely into the third week. They toured for three weeks and opened at the St Martin's Theatre on 11 October 1938. The play was an enormous success and all concerned – author, director, technical staff and cast – won the highest accolades. Not least of these went to my mother.

Good as they are, however, there is no better performance in the play than that of a new discovery, Patricia Hayes, as a housemaid breathing defiance and girlish curiosity with the richest Yorkshire accent.

Daily Sketch

Patricia Hayes, a newcomer, plays a little serving-maid with a rare sense of comedy. This little Yorkshire girl, gauche, direct, full of a queer, blunt literal-mindedness, is the most amusing character in the play. Miss Hayes gives an extraordinarily good performance.

Daily Mail

Shortly after the opening of the play, the actor Frank Pettingell, who played the photographer, was involved in a car accident; his part, which included a long scene with my mother, was played at short notice by Priestley himself. According to my mother, Priestley was a hopeless actor, but the publicity was good for the show! (Another point of interest is that *When We Are Married* became the first play to be televised live, and my mother was in it. According to Basil Dean's autobiography, *Mind's Eye*, it was a major operation fraught with technical difficulties.)

Up until that time, Patricia had represented herself and had no agent. One night after the show Basil Dearden, the company manager, was approached by Herbert de Leon, who asked him if the young Miss Hayes had an agent. Basil mentioned it to Patricia the next day: 'Herbert de Leon told me to tell you that if you ever want an agent, he would be happy to have you on his books. I don't know how good he is as an agent, but he is a very honourable man.' She stored that piece of information for a later date.

A film of *When We Are Married* was made during the War, and Patricia was in it. In 1987, nearly fifty years later, she was in the new production at the Whitehall Theatre, directed by Ron Eyre. This time she played Mrs Northrop, the charwoman – but we will come to that later.

Another piece of very early television that Patricia appeared in was a programme of short excerpts from Shakespeare's plays. She was in an extract from *A Midsummer Night's Dream*, involving Puck and Oberon. My mother played Puck and her Oberon was Alexander Knox, who later emigrated to the USA and became a well-known American film actor.

'Alexander Knox was a great one for coming out with the wrong word during a scene,' she says. 'Unfortunately, he came out with the wrong word in the sentence "My gentle Puck come hither" ' – we need say no more!

'I met him a few years afterwards and he was in a Bernard Shaw play. I reminded him of the occasion when he had slipped up at the rehearsal for *Midsummer Night's Dream* and he said, "I am still doing it. During the play I am in at the moment, someone announces the arrival of Generalissimo Flanco. My next line is, 'Quite so – you are very welcome. Please be seated.' Last night I said, 'Klite so – you are velly weercul.' By that time I knew I was into it and was determined to get the last sentence right, but I heard myself saying, "Plea be slated." '

Valentine Rooke, meanwhile, had found himself a job which suited his frame of mind at that time. He had accepted the position of announcer with Radio Luxembourg. It was not taxing and yet it was steady employment. The year was 1939.

While he was out in Luxembourg, he went to see his German ex-girlfriend, Heidi, and found that she was happily married with two children. Valentine then asked Patricia to marry him.

She accepted without a moment's hesitation, even though it meant coming out of *When We Are Married*. She admits that she had been in it for six months, and was getting tired of it. A career alone would never have satisfied her; and she had always found the relationship with Val so challenging, because he was not keen to make a commitment!

They were married from her parents' flat in Grape Street, and it was a very happy day. Then they were off to Luxembourg for the beginning of their married life.

6

War & Wild Strawberries

There was an uneasy peace in Europe at that time. The previous year had seen the Munich Crisis, after which Chamberlain returned from Germany waving his piece of paper and declaring, 'War has been averted! Peace in our time!'

The first thing that Valentine and Patricia had to do on arrival in Luxembourg was to find themselves an apartment. This took a while, since their priorities were rather different: he was only concerned with the view, whereas my mother was looking for more practical necessities. Eventually they found a flat that met the requirements of them both. As it was unfurnished, they went out and bought new furniture – and soon it was looking pretty and homely, filled with all their recent wedding presents.

They had a ready-made social life since the small community of English-speaking people banded together and entertained themselves frequently and Val had made a lot of friends in the first few months in Luxembourg on his own. At times they would explore the surrounding countryside on their bicycles. One sunny afternoon they were out cycling, when Patricia spotted some particularly succulent and large wild strawberries. Unfortunately they were behind a fence, but there were no 'No Entry' signs – so she decided to climb the fence and pick the strawberries. After all, they were only wild strawberries. Val was more cautious and told her, 'Listen, I don't think you should go in there. It may be part of the Maginot Line.' (The Maginot Line was a line of defences, mainly underground, designed to stop the Germans ever advancing into France again. It extended for many miles along the north-east border of France and Luxembourg. When the war came it proved to be pretty useless and an enormous waste of money, but at that time it was sacred.)

My mother was so enjoying picking the strawberries that she failed to notice Valentine had suddenly gone into hiding. A very large soldier had loomed up from nowhere, and was standing right over her. 'Val – where are you?' she croaked. He emerged from his hiding place.

'What are you doing here?' asked the soldier in German. Val, who was absolutely fluent in French and German, spluttered, 'No speak German.'

'We are English. My husband works in Luxembourg for Radio Luxembourg. We are just picking strawberries.'

'Come with me!'

The large soldier took them to a nearby building where there was an office, and two more soldiers. The population of Luxembourg speak German, French and a local patois called 'Letzeburgesch', but none of the soldiers spoke English, so while Val played dumb, my mother managed to explain why they were there, in her extremely inadequate schoolgirl French. The soldiers probably telephoned Radio Luxembourg to check up on Val, and – whatever the reason – they eventually released them, after explaining that it was indeed the Maginot Line, and that it was absolutely forbidden to trespass there!

Once they were safely outside, Val turned to Patricia. 'I don't know how you managed that! Other people who have been caught near here have been arrested and thoroughly investigated.'

During their stay in Luxembourg, Patricia played the role of housewife although being so very far away from the coast and the sea made her feel land-locked and gave her a degree of claustrophobia. Despite the fact that she was already showing signs of morning sickness, she was very excited when she received a message offering her a part in another West End play. Val was also very encouraging to her, so during his next leave they returned to London together. The month was September, 1939. While they were in England, the Germans bombed Poland, and, true to their promise, the British declared war on Germany.

There was no way that Patricia and Valentine could return to Luxembourg. They lost all their possessions, though it is only fair to add that the Luxembourg government wrote to them after the war, saying that they realized that they had been residents when war was declared, and asking them to estimate the value of their loss. They were reimbursed for the whole sum, about £300, a great deal of money in those days.

As soon as war broke out Val enlisted and applied for a commission – he had been in the OCTU (Officer Cadets Training Unit) at his public school. In many ways he was unsuited to being an officer, because he did not like having to take responsibility for the lives of other men. My mother felt that, with his flair for languages, he would have been much better suited to Intelligence work; his clown-like ways would have thrown people off the scent, and made them unable to believe that he was spying.

Once Valentine had enlisted, he was sent to an OCTU base in Colchester to do his training. No army wives were allowed there. Patricia, meanwhile, went to see Herbert de Leon, the agent who had shown an interest in her during *When We Are Married*. She had been offered a part in a play being put on by the Gilbert Miller Management, and this time she wanted someone experienced to negotiate her money for her. Thus began a lifetime's association: Herbert de Leon took her on to his books, and she has been there ever since. He died a few years back, but his wife Hazel took over and represents my mother to this day.

There would come a time, years later, when my mother

worked frequently with many of the famous English comedians. This often involved appearing in television shows, with a live audience, which would be recorded at one television theatre or other.

After the show was over, it was normal for some audience members to stay behind hoping to collect autographs from the actors. However, my mother began to notice that there was one woman who always seemed to be there, and was always staring at her. At first my mother was flattered, but after a while she began to feel a little uneasy. Surely no normal person would be so obsessed? From then onwards my mother did everything she could to avoid the woman, deliberately walking in the opposite direction when she saw her coming. She was absolutely horrified, one evening, when the crowd was dense, and she realized that she could not escape and that the woman was catching up with her at an alarming rate. My mother braced herself and turned around to face the monster.

'At last, I've got to meet you,' said the woman.

'Who are you?' asked my mother, bravely.

'I'm your agent,' said Hazel de Leon. They had never met!

However, back in 1940, my mother, heavily pregnant, found herself a flat in Brighton and commuted for any radio work that she was offered. The flat consisted of the basement that ran right underneath a very large house in Arundel Terrace. Her mother and father were looking for an apartment, too, and, as this one divided very easily into two self-contained areas, they all moved in together. One of the attractions of the flat was that it had a very large wine-cellar, which would have been a marvellous spot if there had been a bad air-raid. Valentine's mother was also living in Brighton, so they were all able to help each other out when necessary.

My brave little mother went up to London frequently for work and travelled back to Brighton, late at night, during the 'black-out'. There would often be air-raids, and she remembers one night in particular. She had arrived at Victoria Station just as the sirens were sounding, and was so terrified that she began to shake from head to foot. A well-known writer, called Monckton Hoffe, and his lady, the actress Grizelda Harvey, were also waiting for the train. 'I'm getting Grizelda a whisky – would you like one?' enquired Mr Hoffe generously.

'No thank you – I never drink,' she managed to reply through her chattering teeth.

When Mr Hoffe returned, he had brought them both a large whisky. 'I think you need this too,' he said.

My mother drank it, and it was wonderful. It relaxed her and she stopped shivering and shaking.

It was at about this time that she visited a doctor regarding her pregnancy; because she was small, the doctor asked her to see a specialist. The specialist – Mr Enwright – told her that she would definitely have to have a Caesarian. 'The baby is big, and your pelvis is not a good shape. Come into hospital two weeks before it is expected.' My mother was very disappointed because she had been looking forward to a natural birth.

Out of the blue, she was asked to go to Manchester to do a radio play. She went by train, and her mother went with her. They stayed in the Midland Hotel. The broadcast went well and she and her mother got safely home. She had only been back a few days when she was telephoned and asked if she could come up again the following week to do another play. She agreed and, this time, her sister Moira was to go with her.

On arrival in Manchester, they arranged to stay in 'digs' with an extremely pleasant, welcoming, north-country woman called Mrs Jackson, to whom my mother, quite unnecessarily, said, 'Actually, I'm having a baby soon.' (She was due in three weeks!)

'Don't worry about that, love. There's been three children born in this house, and none of them mine. In every case, at the last moment, we rushed them off to St Mary's Hospital to have the baby there. Everything will be fine,' said Mrs Jackson, very reassuringly. My mother did not actually need reassuring; in her naïvety she thought that because the baby was due in three weeks' time, that was when it would come!

The next day Gladys Young, who had also been in the broadcast, saw Patricia and Moira on to the train. They had sleepers. Afterwards Gladys told my mother, 'I have never been so glad to see the back of anybody as I was to see the back of you. I thought you were going to have the baby in the Studio!'

'I didn't think it possible, I hadn't completed the nine months!' said Patricia.

The train got into London at 5.30 a.m. The guard who looked after the sleepers asked my mother what time they wanted to be called, and she said 7 a.m. The train to Brighton left at 8 a.m.

My mother turned over to get some more sleep. She awoke suddenly, and could hear the sound of water running, as if someone had left a tap on. It dawned on her finally that her waters had broken and the water was pouring from the bunk on to the floor.

When she realized what was happening, she woke Moira. 'I think I'm going to have the baby!'

'What shall I do?' asked Moira, desperately.

'Get out of the train – walk down the platform – and find the first official, a porter or a policeman, and tell him that I'm in the carriage and that I'm going to have the baby any minute.'

Poor Moira rushed off down the platform, and the first person that she bumped into was a policeman. 'When I saw that young lady coming down the platform, I thought, here comes somebody full of trouble,' remarked the policeman, much later.

'Now then – what's all this about you having a baby?' he asked Patricia, on his arrival in the carriage. 'Oh yes – you are having it,' he said, as he shone his torch on the floor and the light gleamed in the pool of water. 'Wait here and we'll get you an ambulance.'

The ambulance came, and she was taken to the nearest hospital, with the policeman and Moira in attendance. A doctor came out. 'I'm sorry, we can't take you in here; we don't have the proper facilities. If you have the baby here you'll have to have it in Casualty. Go to St Mary's in Islington; they have a maternity ward there. I'll send a nurse with you who has done midwifery.'

So off they went again, with the policeman and the nurse grumbling to Moira about how disgusting it was that they would not admit her at the hospital. When they arrived at St Mary's, she was taken quickly to the labour ward. She was admitted and comfortably in the ward at 7 a.m.

Suddenly there was a change of atmosphere as the day-staff came on duty. The ward was bristling with activity. As one of the nurses flashed by, my mother ventured, 'I'm supposed to be having a Caesarian.'

'Don't worry, if you need a Caesarian you will get one here – Miss Hill will do it!'

'Miss Hill! Who is Miss Hill?' wondered my mother. It did not occur to her that a Miss Hill could be a qualified doctor and surgeon. Who were they going to let loose on her?

'Are you getting any pains?' cross-examined a fierce Sister.

'Every now and then I get a faint twinge.' Having heard about the terrible pains of childbirth, she decided not to worry about them until they were there. She had watched a cat having kittens once and noticed that it was relaxed and purring; every now and then its eyes would dilate in shock and horror, then the spasm would pass away and it would continue to purr as though nothing had happened.

So my mother relaxed and hoped against hope that she would not have to have a Caesarian.

'Turn on your side,' commanded the fierce Sister. 'Next time you have a pain try a little push.'

Six pushes later the baby was born.

'He's here,' said the Sister in true amazement. Patricia had given birth very easily, and there was Richard, boxing his way into life.

When I was born eighteen months later, in a Blackpool nursing home, the doctor commented, 'It's not having babies with you, Mrs Brooke, it's bullets out of a gun!'

Richard was a very sleepy baby and a little jaundiced, because he was early. However, my mother persevered with the breast-feeding in the hospital, under the care and supervision of the midwives. One day, she had just finished feeding Richard, when a rather harassed nurse asked her to feed a premature baby, whose mother was unable to feed him. Patricia took the poor little thing into her arms and proceeded to breast-feed him.

A few minutes later the nurse reappeared, with a bottle of milk in her hand. 'What are you doing, Mother?' she demanded, aghast.

'I am feeding the baby, as you asked me,' replied my mother innocently.

'Not that way, Mother – I only went away to get you the bottle!'

Richard spent the first few months of his life in Brighton, then in Edinburgh, when Valentine was transferred there to continue his training. But the war years are extremely difficult to piece together. People moved around frequently, for a variety of reasons. Many, particularly women and children, were evacuated from London to places that were considered safer. Unmarried men and women either enlisted or were called up to serve their country. The confusion must have been enormous. My mother remembers events as though they were yesterday, but finds it difficult to remember the sequence of happenings.

Valentine was eventually sent to India with Draft 'RAYOF' (a code-name used to deceive the enemy), as a replacement in the Lincolnshire Regiment. He remained there for three and a half years, until the war was over.

Patricia's father was posted to Blackpool with the Civil Service; he could not enlist because of his deafness. Her mother spent her time between Blackpool and wherever my mother was, helping her with the children when she was working.

Moira, who had been acting with Eric Phillip's Repertory Company at Westcliff-on-Sea, returned to London and noticed that the WAAF was advertising for recruits to do 'Special Duties'. She felt the need to enlist, and the idea of Special Duties appealed to her. When she went for her interview, there were three officers, two women and a man, sitting at a table.

'You look to me to be a little highly strung,' commented the man and Moira replied, 'I'm a bit nervous at interviews, but I'm all right in an emergency.'

'Why – what emergency have you been in?' he asked.

'Well – my sister had a baby on a train.'

He did not seem very impressed, but the female WAAF officers laughed and one said, 'Oh dear, that *was* an emergency!'

She was accepted for Special Duties and became a plotter at Tangmere Airfield, which was bombed during the Battle of Britain. Moira describes it thus: 'We were at dinner in the WAAF's mess, when a voice came loudly over the Tannoy. "A large number of enemy aircraft are approaching the Airfield. Take cover – take *cover*." Everyone rushed out and into the air-raid shelters, which were just long trenches, covered over with corrugated iron. Within a few minutes we heard planes flying low, and then bombs exploding. Then the "all clear" came and we emerged to see the parade ground a mass of concrete and rock. There was more damage, but we were not told how much, nor were we encouraged to find out. As we went on watch a bit later (the operations room had not been hit) I passed a dead airman lying on the ground, and that upset me, but it all happened so quickly that I hadn't time to be frightened.'

Although she enjoyed the work at Tangmere, Moira applied for a transfer to India, to do Photographic Intelligence work. When I asked my mother why Moira had applied for the transfer, she told me it was because she realized that a young Canadian based at Tangmere was falling in love with her. He had a wife and two children in Canada, and Moira did not want

Patricia as Moth in *Love's Labours Lost*. Stratford, 1934.

With Peter Ridgeway in *Charles and Mary* in the early Players Theatre days.

Appearing as Dora in *Night Must Fall*. Cambridge Theatre, 1936.

Patricia as Min Lee in an Edgar Wallace thriller.

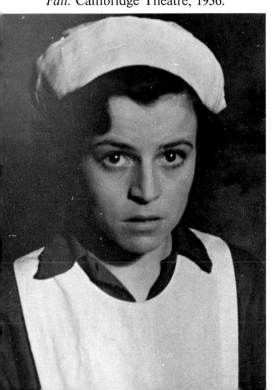

Wedding day, 10 June 1939, Patricia and her father about to enter the church, St Patrick's, Soho Square.

The happy wedding party.

Appearing with J B Priestley during the run of *When We Are Married*.

George and Florence Hayes with Jemima in Colwyn Bay, 1940.

What a handful we must have been! Patricia with toddler Teresa and tricyclist Richard in wartime Washington, Sussex.

Daughter Gemma with her beloved doll named, very simply, 'Wer'!

to be the cause of a break-up.

Apparently New Delhi, where Moira was transferred to, was so far from any action (the theatre of war was in Burma) that she led an almost peacetime existence with other Service personnel, with RAF, Army, and Americans in abundance. The only scarcity was of white women! Parties were frequent, Indian servants were supplied, Indian tailors made civilian clothes, and no coupons were required. When Moira wrote to Patricia she was obviously amazed at the completely different way of life and attitudes of the people in India:

> In England we do everything for ourselves. In India, we leave the bed unmade – step out of our clothes and leave them lying on the floor. The servants do it all. They are lovely, gentle, and dignified people, very poor, but they wear their rags like royalty.

The life of luxury did not last very long for Moira because she met Gordon Dixon, an officer from the Royal Warwickshire Regiment, and six months later they were married. Moira wrote to my father in Burma and asked him to give her away, because she felt sad to be getting married with no family around. He managed to get leave and, as Moira says, he was probably glad to be able to escape from the Army for a few days.

Brian, Patricia's brother, had been working with various repertory companies around England, but he was eventually called up and June followed him, getting 'digs' wherever he was stationed. People were moved around a great deal when they were being trained. Eventually, when Peter, their first child, was due to be born, June went back to her parents in Wilmslow near Manchester and remained there until the war was over. When the war turned in favour of the British and their allies, and the invasion of France was planned, Brian's 'Anti-Tank' Regiment, in which he was now a Captain, was sent to Northern Ireland. As Fortune would have it, when the offensive began, Brian was in hospital being operated on for haemorroids and he missed the fighting. There cannot be many people who have welcomed that very uncomfortable operation! After the war he was sent to Germany as part of the Army of Occupation.

My grandparents lived in digs in Blackpool, because my grandfather needed someone to take care of him whenever Florence was away helping my mother. The landladies that the family stayed with in Blackpool must have been a great source of comedy material, stored by my mother for a later date. For example, there was Miss Monaghan, a Blackpool-Irishwoman. She did not approve of the rather Bohemian ways of some of the evacuees from the south. She would say disapprovingly: 'Those new people next door are Londoners. They have not had their curtains down since they came here – it's six months!'

'How often should they come down?' asked my mother, sincerely. 'When do you take yours down?'

'I wait while the Earnshaws opposite take theirs down, then I take mine down,' said Miss Monaghan religiously.

'Why have you dressed Richard in blue?' she asked one day, and then qualified it by adding, 'It's blue for a girl and it's pink for a boy.' My mother saw absolutely no point in disputing with Miss Monaghan; it never paid off.

Surprisingly enough, my mother worked quite frequently during the war. Apart from her usual quota of radio work, she made two films: *Went The Day Well?* with Lesley Banks, and *Great Day* with Eric Portman.

Went The Day Well? was directed by the important Brazilian director, Alberto Cavalcanti. He was extremely helpful to my mother. Knowing that she was primarily a stage actress, he would put his hand on her shoulder before each take and say, 'Don't act – just think. Stage and film techniques are quite different.'

During the making of *Great Day* my mother was complaining about the fact that she had to hang about for several days to do her small bit of filming. She wanted to get home to her little ones. 'You should never complain,' Lance Comfort the director said to her. 'You are one of those fortunate women who have the best of both worlds. Not many women can be married with children and also have a very interesting and exciting career. Don't grumble – you are very lucky!'

The war was to get a lot worse before it got better. Even when the Germans realized that they were no longer winning, they started a huge campaign of bombing in order to try to lower the morale of the English. The bombing must have been terrifying. It was almost better to be in the Army than to be a sitting duck, waiting for the bombs to drop.

My Mother stayed sometimes with Inga the Danish wife of Derek Baker, who had been a Radio Luxembourg announcer with Val, in his mother's house just outside Croydon, in Shirley. One day my mother looked up and suddenly said, 'In the daytime, when you look up at the sky, and the enormous size of it, you realize that the chances of a bomb falling on to your house are very remote. There is no point in worrying.'

Patricia used to be able to see the Bakers' house from the train window when she was travelling to London from Brighton. One day, as she was on her way to Town, she thought, 'Where's the Baker's house?' Coming back she looked again but couldn't see it. Shortly afterwards she received a letter from Derek's wife. 'Our house suffered a direct hit. Derek and I survived, but we've lost the baby. She was killed by the blast.'

During that time my mother bought her first house. The price was £850. Her father had just received his gratuity, so he lent her £300 to go with the £550 she had saved. She managed to repay her father within a year.

That house was in Washington, Sussex, and my earliest memories were formed there. I remember my mother being ill with flu and thinking that having 'flu' meant that she was going to fly. I was really worried that she would fly away. She kept chickens in the garden and we used to go with her to fetch the warm, freshly laid eggs. In the winter she would mix up a little milk with sugar and stand it on the doorstep overnight, the next day that was our ice-cream. There were the blackout boards that had to be up in front of the windows each night. Nearby there was a children's playground where she first taught me the joy of swinging. Even now I can recapture the smell of the Washington house and picture my mother in the lounge, wearing her green Paisley dressing-gown.

7

Sadness & Joy

The celebrations at the end of the Second World War must have been ecstatic. However, when the excitement had died down, Britain was faced with the grim reality of the devastation that the war had caused. Many of the major cities had been reduced to a heap of rubble. The country was virtually bankrupt, and the problems were not over. The leaders of the victorious countries were trying to decide how to apportion the spoils, and work out exactly what to do with the defeated Germans and Japanese to ensure that they would never be able to cause another World War.

Meanwhile the troops were being demobilized, and many men returned home to live with wives and children who were virtually strangers. The women had, of necessity, become alarmingly independent. They did not suddenly want to be told what to do; they had learned to manage on their own and most of them liked it. A very conventional neighbour of my mother's in London, seemingly in the happiest of marriages, said recently that it was a miracle that she and her husband had stayed together immediately after the war; there was really no place for her husband in the home on his return. The women felt resentful and the men felt inadequate.

Valentine admitted to my mother that he found it difficult to handle the fact that on his return the vulnerable young wife he had had to abandon to go to India was a thriving house-owner, quite capable of maintaining herself and their two children. My brother Richard and I were complete strangers to him, and we probably resented the fact that this unknown person required so much of our mother's attention. He was also unused to the deprivations of civilian life; the Army in India had always had enough to eat, as well as being waited on hand and foot by servants.

The strangest problem that arose between Valentine and Patricia was the least expected. Valentine had become a convert to Catholicism. You may well wonder why this should have been a problem; surely this would have been my mother's dearest wish! However, when people have grown up within a faith, they take it in their stride; it is no big deal, they behave like anybody else, except when reacting to major issues which are not the order of the day. Their religion is as much a normal part of their lives as eating or breathing. Converts, on the other hand, are notorious for their burning religious fervour and my mother found this extremely difficult to live with. 'You only had to open a door, and you would find Val on his knees on the other side of it.'

He desperately tried to make my mother more religious. He wanted her to say the rosary with him, rather than listen to the radio or play bridge. Sometimes, if she refused to spend more time on her knees praying, he would visit their parish priest, looking for support. The priest very sensibly told him that charity was more important than any other virtue, and that out of charity he should listen to the radio or play bridge with my mother and say his rosary on his own, at another time, when she did not need his company. 'It's no use trying to make me become more pious,' Patricia told him. 'I'm not pious by nature. I do other things.'

As soon as the war was over, Brian was sent to Germany with the Army of Occupation. On hearing that he was going, Valentine approached him: 'Would you try and find out what has happened to the family of an ex-girlfriend of mine, Heidi?'

Brian agreed, and eventually found his way to where they lived. He went to see Heidi, her husband, two children and

family. He reported back to Val that they were all safe, and
that Heidi was happily married to a judge.

Brian came out of the Army shortly before he was due to
be demobilized because John Clements offered him a part in
a play he was putting on in the West End. Brian and June
bought a two-bedroom house in Brighton and he travelled up
and down to London to work.

My mother was still living in the cottage in Washington,
but as Richard was now of school age, and there was no
longer any threat of air-raids, she and Valentine started to
look for a house to rent in Brighton. She noticed that a
requisitioned house in Upper Drive was now empty; Val
wrote to the local Council and three weeks later they were
able to move in. Moira and Gordon rented her cottage in
Washington and stayed there for the next eight years.

Employment was a very real problem for Valentine. He
was determined never to go back to acting. He had no
qualifications, apart from his drama training at RADA.
However, after a series of very unsatisfactory positions, he
noticed a newspaper announcement that men who'd held
posts such as his could apply to rejoin the Army and work
for the Control Commission in Germany.

He jumped at the chance, and as soon as he arrived in
Germany he could not resist looking up Heidi. How things
had changed! Apparently, by this time, Heidi and her
husband were apart, and seeking annulment of their marriage
from the Catholic Church, on the grounds that it had been
arranged, and imposed on them by their parents. Heidi was
thrilled to see Valentine – suddenly there was someone to
look after her, a gallant Major from the British Army who
could help to provide the basic necessities that were almost
impossible for the average German citizen to obtain.

It was inevitable that my father and Heidi re-kindled the
fires of their original relationship. She now needed him
desperately, and he felt like a hero, finally able to win the
approval of the woman he had loved in vain just a few years
previously. It must have seemed to him that my mother was

well able to cope without him, and that Heidi's very life was in danger without his protection. What he failed to appreciate was that my mother still loved him, and considered that she was married to him for life. During the war, when Washington was filled with handsome, wealthy Canadian soldiers, she had been one of the few women in the village who had remained completely faithful.

My mother was devastated when she received a letter from Val in Germany telling her that he'd gone back to Heidi, and that he had applied to Rome for an annulment of their marriage. Heidi wrote, too, saying, 'I hope you understand that I am not taking him from you, it is just that I did not realize at the time how much I really loved him!'

It would have been totally out of character for my mother to let him go without a fight. She loved him, and she had two children who needed their father. She fought him on every level, but the Catholic religion (which had been causing problems within their marriage, due to his recent and overwhelming conversion) suddenly became her strongest ally. No matter how he argued, which priests or bishops he went to see, he could not convince any of them that he was in the right. In the eyes of the Church he was married to my mother, and that was that.

He returned to England for a reconciliation, during which time my sister Gemma was conceived; but ultimately he left my mother for good, with the parting words: 'I cannot leave the woman I love to starve to death in Germany.' In fairness, he did remain with Heidi until her recent death.

The following revelation is light relief to the ghastliness of this tragedy. My mother says, 'After he had gone, instead of breaking down and crying, I walked towards a mirror on the wall and I looked at my face and thought – Yes – I must remember that – this is the face of a woman who has just been abandoned by her husband. If I have to act such a woman in a play I will know exactly how to be. Similarly, when I was a child, I would sometimes have a big scene with my mother which ended in tears, and I can remember thinking to myself, when I was quite young, that I had got to that stage in my crying when no more tears would come, but I was kind of gasping for breath and dry-crying. I used to think – I must remember this for when I'm in a play and playing the part of someone who is desperately, desperately crying and now has got to pull themselves together and get over it!'

Many people who knew my mother at that time remember how overwhelmingly unhappy she was. What strength of character it showed that she was able to carry on, although she admits that to her, unlike most women, the prospect of rearing three children, and maintaining them on her own, was not a daunting one. She welcomed and enjoyed responsibility. However the loneliness must have been bleak and empty.

A few months later, my mother gave birth to my sister, Gemma. What a joy she proved to be. My brother and I had always been very naughty, up to any pranks we could think of, but at this devastating time in her life my mother gave birth to a 'good' child. Gemma lay in her pram and smiled, hardly ever crying. She worshipped Richard and myself, watching us adoringly as we raced around her, creating havoc and destruction. It was as though Gemma had been sent to my mother as a compensation for her sad loss. She called her her 'consolation prize'.

For the next few years we continued to live in the Brighton house, at 60 Upper Drive. Off Dyke Road, it stood right next to the Convent of the Sacred Heart – the same religious order who had taught my mother, and trained my grandmother to be a teacher. Our garden had a high wall built in Sussex stone, and if we climbed up and looked over it we could gaze into the beautifully manicured Convent grounds. Richard and I both went to school there, when we were tiny.

My grandparents had by then bought a house in College Road, Brighton, and whenever my mother was working, one or other would come over and take care of us. I remember one day my grandfather was minding us, and for some reason he wanted to go up to the attic. The entrance to the attic was through a trapdoor in the upstairs landing ceiling. He found a ladder and positioned it so that he had access and then proceeded to go up and down the ladder a few times to complete his purpose; but he made the mistake of leaving the ladder in the hall when he had finished. Richard and I (Gemma was too little) decided to explore the attic. We climbed up successfully but, when we turned around a few minutes later to come down again, we were horrified to discover that he had removed the ladder. Because of his deafness he could not hear our anxious cries. How worried he must have been on discovering that we seemed to have disappeared! Fortunately my mother returned not too much later, and we were rescued from the attic – and severely reprimanded.

8

The Boy/Girl

Now, more than ever, my mother needed to earn good money; but she also wanted to spend as much time as possible with her children. In the curious way that Fate so often takes a hand, it was her career in radio that prospered at that time. Broadcasting was absolutely ideal for her way of life. As long as she had two or three jobs a month she could manage comfortably, and she did not have to tour or work late every night. Her mother or father would always look after the children in order for her to work, which meant that she was not obliged to afford expensive nannies; and, just as importantly, she never felt as if she was leaving her beloved brood with strangers.

Ever since her season at Stratford-on-Avon, my mother had been renowned for her ability to play boys. She played many, many boys on the radio. Her reading is quite phenomenal; she can pick up a script and, on a first reading, give an almost perfect interpretation of a role. She has sometimes warned theatre producers that she will not recapture the brilliance of her first reading until her hundredth performance!

No real boy was allowed to work until he was twelve years old, and then he had to have a licence and a chaperone. The Children's Hour programmes were done in a day. The cast arrived at the studio at about 11 a.m. and the programme went out live at 5.15 p.m. Not many boys were capable of reading and acting in a convincing way in such a short time. Therefore numerous producers would far rather have my mother, who was experienced and reliable, than a real boy. It became an absolute speciality. She perfected it, and she sounded exactly like a boy. The voice and mannerisms were probably based on her memory of her brother Brian as a child.

One of the programmes in which she could be heard regularly as a boy was 'Norman and Henry Bones, the Boy Detectives' by Antony C. Wilson, which went out on BBC Children's Hour. The producer was Josephine Plummer. It was a series about the adventures of two young boys: Norman Bones, a lad of about sixteen, nearly always played by Charles Hawtrey, and his younger cousin, Henry, aged eleven, played by my mother. Both Charles and Patricia were in their thirties! My mother says:

'Charles Hawtrey played Norman in a style all his own. He sounded slightly professional, like that rather intellectual sort of boy with horn-rimmed spectacles, who thinks everything out very cleverly. Henry was the complete, but enthusiastic, naïve schoolboy, dying for adventures. Charles and I threw ourselves into the spirit of the plot with great enthusiasm and enjoyed it enormously. Denholm Elliott took over for a couple of episodes when Charles was in one of the 'Carry On' films, but he seemed to feel rather foolish playing Norman Bones.'

The stories were quite complicated and often very exciting. We used to listen to it with my grandfather. Oddly, when my mother returned home after the broadcast she had not the faintest idea of the storyline and would always ask us exactly what had happened in the frightfully complicated plot. With the amazing clearmindedness of youth, we would have deciphered the story, answering perhaps, 'It was easy to understand, Mummy, the stolen jewels were hidden in the stuffed owl at the old antique shop, and when Mr Dimmity bent down to tie up his shoe lace, at the Rectory, and noticed that the stuffed owl, which had been borrowed by the Vicar for the Church Fete, had a glint in its eye ...' And so on, and so forth.

The series was a great success; but my mother remembers that, one day, a friend of hers introduced her to two women friends as Patricia Hayes, the well-known actress. 'These women were about my age,' says my mother. 'When they were told that I played Henry in 'Norman and Henry Bones' one of the women looked at me and said, "You don't mean to say that you are one of those ghastly little boys!" I was waiting for her to say, "One of those two marvellous detectives". It just shows how sometimes fame is not because you are good, but because you are bad! It's good for one, though, from time to time, to be taken down a peg.'

She had become one of the most sought-after radio actresses of the day. One producer confided in my mother, 'I have become terribly lazy. As soon as I get a script, I write your name against all the women's parts, any children's parts and any birds or animals. Then I set to and cast the men!'

Apparently my mother could imitate cats and canaries, children crying, babies, goats, lambs. Nowadays it would not be allowed; Equity would probably step in and insist that the animal sound effects were done by an expert, especially paid to perform that job, but in those days she was allowed to do it all.

The Features Department of the BBC contacted her one day, asking her to be in a regular radio series starring Wilfred Pickles, called 'Ex-Corporal Wilf'. It was extremely appropriate for the times, because it was a fifteen-minute duologue between an ex-Corporal (played by Wilfred Pickles), who had just got out of the Army and his wife (my mother) who had been at home. It showed how the wife had got used to ruling the roost and having control over the money. The message was an extremely serious one, but it was given comedy treatment.

Pat Dixon, who was in charge of Light Entertainment, rang her and said, 'I've just been listening to you in 'Ex-Corporal Wilf', and I'm sure that you would do very well in Light Entertainment. Do you think you could cope with doing broadcast sketches and playing them to a live audience at the same time?'

'Yes – I'm sure I could. Before the war, most of what I did was theatre work,' my mother told him.

She was immediately contracted for fourteen weeks, to be in a programme, written by Max Wall, called 'Our Shed'. The scripts were very amusing, her character always wanted to agree with the Max Wall character; for example, she might talk about something she liked, he would reveal that it was something that he hated and immediately afterwards she would agree with him that she hated it too.

In September 1948 my mother moved from Brighton to a large three-storey Victorian house in Wandsworth. Forty years later she is still there. One of the reasons for the move was to be near the schools which she wanted us to attend, and another was that most of her work was in London. We joined my mother at the new house a week after she had moved in. I remember rushing out into the large garden and discovering the rocky lily pond with a fountain, which was hastily filled in by my grandfather for safety. Shortly after we moved in Patricia put up a chicken-run adjoining the garden shed, and bought some day-old chicks. A few months later we once again had delicious new-laid eggs. A swing was erected in the garden, and a slide and a jungle gym. There were some mature fruit trees, among them an old Worcester Pearmain which annually produced a magnificent crop of crisp, green and crimson apples. The windfalls were loaded into baskets by my mother and placed on the front fence under the beech tree for passers-by to help themselves. We had a dog called Tyko who as a stray had followed me home from the market in Brighton when we were shopping there; she had given such a pleading look as we jumped on the bus to go home, that my mother encouraged her on to the bus with us. Her remains and her headstone are now under the Worcester Pearmain. The crab-apple tree, with fruit that looked like cherries, was also laden every year. The crab-apples were used by Richard and me as scarlet missiles to be dispatched from behind the cover of the low wall enclosing the flat roof at passing cars. I think we were rather encouraged in our mischief when my mother had told us that, as children, she and her brother and sister had amused themselves by popping small potatoes into the rims of people's hats from the top of their garden wall.

It was at about this time that she bought, and taught us to ride, our bicycles. What a lively little family we must have been! We children began to make friends, for ourselves and my mother, in no time. Richard and William Culver, two doors up, tore round the neighbourhood on their bicycles. They taught me to descend the steep Skeena Hill, not only without holding the handlebars, but even standing up on the saddle. The worst prank they got up to was when they took their catapults into the garden shed and fired hundreds of stones through a hole in the roof. It was not until neighbours became suspicious, after thirty-two windows in the area had been broken, that they were discovered!

Patricia took us to church every Sunday and to Stations of the Cross on Good Friday. Later we enjoyed the excitement of wrapping up warmly and walking down, through the snow or frost, to Midnight Mass on Christmas Eve in the pretty little Convent chapel that was filled with candles and the smell of incense, in the knowledge that we had reduced the long wait until morning when we could open the laden stockings on our beds. She always gave us lovely presents, dolls and clockwork trains and building bricks. We had by far the best dressing-up box of anyone we knew.

In order to supplement her income in those early days, she would sometimes rent out the top floor, at a very reasonable rent. There were three delightful Irish nurses, aunts of a school friend of mine, who lived there at one time. Pat, Gret and Lil Nolan were their names. They liked clothes, and as it was the days when a woman had to wear a hat to church, they had a wide selection of hats. From time to time, they would have a huge clear-out, and the dustbin would be filled with clothes, laddered stockings, shoes and – of course – hats that were no longer the favourites. I wonder if the nurses ever knew that as soon as they had gone off to work in the morning, after one of their clearouts, my mother would descend on the dustbin like a ravaging vulture? Most of her spoils went straight into our dressing-up box; but frequently she would appear as a comedy character on television, wearing one of the Nolans' hats!

Shortly after my mother's move to London, Brian and June and their four sons – Peter, Michael, Timothy and Hugh – moved to Wimbledon. They also purchased a large, three-storey Victorian house with a wonderful garden, which ran right down to the railway and was filled with the most magnificent fruit trees: apples, greengages, damsons and Victoria plums. We spent many a happy day there in the summer helping to harvest the fruit, and trying to avoid being stung by the wasps whose interest in the plums seemed to be even greater than our own.

Auntie Moira and Gordon were still in the Washington house. Gordon was a bank manager and it was not long before he was transferred to Worthing, where they later moved with their two children, John and Gina.

Every summer my grandparents went to Ireland and, as the grandchildren grew older, they began to rent a large property for the holidays and make us all welcome. What wonderful holidays they were! Rather like my grandfather when he was a boy, all the cousins were able to run wild through the countryside in complete safety. One year they leased a mansion called Glenally House in Youghal. It was an old Georgian manor in the most unbelievable state of disrepair, set in huge overgrown grounds. In front of the oval driveway, there was a large field which was bordered by a stream. Behind the house there was an orchard. The drawing-room had brown peeling wallpaper, broken chandeliers, black with dirt, an amazingly out-of-tune piano and valuable antique furniture with surfaces ruined by the damp that had not been treated for at least twenty-five years.

Patricia and her old friend Leonard Sachs in a Sunday night show at the Players Theatre.

Eamonn Andrews asks Patricia and Charles Hawtrey to recall their 'Norman and Henry Bones' radio days.

Saying: 'Not until after six o'clock' to Ted Ray in 'Ray's-a-Laugh', 1951

The 'gang' during rehearsals for 'Ray's-a-Laugh'.

Each of the many bedrooms had a giant four-poster bed, heavy with torn and bedraggled drapes and choked with ancient cobwebs. The roof leaked in many places, and cooking on the archaic kitchen equipment must have been a nightmare for the adults. However, to us children it was a dark, damp, rambling, haunted paradise. We slept together in the enormous beds – we were too nervous of bogeymen to sleep alone. We played hide-and-seek everywhere, both inside and out, and when the weather was good we climbed into the car and were driven to the beach to swim. My mother would join us for as long as she was free, and she was always more relaxed and happy with all the family than struggling on her own with us in London.

George Innes, the radio producer, came to see my mother in 'Our Shed' one day, and signed her up straightaway with a six-week contract in 'Ray's-a-Laugh', Ted Ray's own comedy programme. She remained in the programme for five and a half years, and it really improved the quality of her life. Now she had a guaranteed income and regular work.

'Ray's-a-Laugh' was a radio show, written by Eddie McGuire, which became one of the most popular comedy shows of the era. It was always performed before a live audience at the Paris Theatre or the Aeolian Hall. The cast would meet at 11 a.m., have a couple of run-throughs, a bite of lunch, tidy things up, then a final rehearsal. At 7 p.m. the audience would be allowed in, and the show would go out live at 7.30.

There was a regular format to the show. First Ted Ray would do what was called 'the audience warm-up' which did not go out on the air; it consisted of Ted telling jokes and, frequently, playing his violin. (He was an extremely accomplished violinist.) Then the show 'proper' went out. The first part consisted of a domestic situation with Kitty Bluett, a well-known Australian actress, playing his wife. The second half of the show involved Ted Ray playing a man called George. George and his Conscience had adventures, during which they met a series of very amusing characters.

These characters would recur week after week, and had some memorable stock phrases. The comedy parts of the programme were interspersed with music provided by Stanley Black and his Orchestra, Bob and Alf Pearson and a group of singers who called themselves 'The Beaux and the Belles'. Pearl Carr and Teddy Johnson, who later branched out on their own as duettists, were among them.

My mother says, 'I was always very grateful to Ted Ray, because I was not very good at first. I did not understand the real music-hall or musical-comedy type of comedy. There are certain techniques: for instance, the feed line (that is the line preceding the gag) must be heard. If I came in with the feed line too early, while the audience were still laughing, Ted would ask, "What did you say?" I would repeat it, and he would say his next line and get the laugh.' She gradually learned, and the knowledge proved invaluable in the later years when she worked consistently with so many of the great English comedians.

Ted Ray was charming and delightful to work with. He was also astute enough to surround himself with a cast of extremely versatile and funny actors: there was Kitty Bluett, a comedienne with a style all her own, Fred Yule, Lesley Perrins (George's Conscience), Patricia Hayes and last, but by no means least, a young actor who was to become a big international star – Peter Sellers.

Peter Sellers joined the cast shortly after my mother, and it was obvious from the start that he had a brilliant talent. The numerous characters he created were all totally original and extremely funny. A source of great inspiration and ingenuity, he assisted the writer, Eddie McGuire, by making suggestions for new characters. One of the characters Peter played was called Crystal Jollybottom. Alas, the character was banned because of the name! He also played a schoolboy whose stock phrase in reply to anyone was, 'And you've got a big red conk!'

This line was also forbidden. It was not considered a good example to children who might be listening, though all the sexual innuendoes and *doubles entendres* in the programme were permitted. My mother's theory is that these went straight over the heads of the powers that be!

Peter Sellers came to rehearsals one day and said, 'Look, I've been offered a part in a film and I was wondering if it would be all right by you, George, and everyone else, if my coach watches the show.'

When she saw Peter the next week, my mother asked him how he was getting on with the film. He replied that it was OK, but that he only had another week until they started shooting. That night he rang her; the first and only time that Peter Sellers ever rang my mother.

'I wonder if you would do me a very great favour, Patricia. Would *you* coach me in this film part?'

'But you've got a coach, Peter.'

'I know I have, but she's not teaching me anything that I don't already know.'

'Well, Peter, neither could I,' my mother replied. 'I'll see you at rehearsals tomorrow, and we can discuss it further.'

When she saw him at the rehearsal she told him, 'Look, Peter, there are certain techniques in film acting, but it is basically the same as any other acting. Your director will tell you what he wants you to do. All *you* need to do is to take your enormous acting talent down to the studios tomorrow, and you'll find that they'll be so grateful that you will get all the help you need with technicalities.'

'Are you sure?' he said desperately. 'I don't mind paying you for some acting lessons.'

'I am absolutely certain that you will be fine,' my mother reassured him. How right she was!

Peter Sellers adored motor cars. In eighteen months he had fifteen different cars. When my mother arrived in Lower Regent Street for the rehearsal every week, she would look to see what fantastic vehicle was parked outside the studio. He owned Jaguars, Rovers, Morgans, Rolls Royces – all the best and most expensive models.

Apparently he found it difficult to deny himself anything

that he saw and took a fancy to; and not just among automobiles. One day he met, in the foyer of the Aeolian Hall, a woman with an adorable little Maltese terrier puppy. Peter went straight up to her. 'Where did you get that dog?'

The next week he arrived at the studio with a dog exactly the same as the one he had seen. He had driven out to the kennels the woman had mentioned, and bought one there and then. 'He only kept it for two weeks, then he got sick of it and gave it to somebody else,' says my mother.

As children, were not allowed to listen to 'Ray's-a-Laugh' which, it was decreed, was on too late for us. However, we used to take advantage of my grandfather's deafness: he had to have the radio volume turned up very loud in order to hear the programme, so we used to creep downstairs, and sit on the floor in the hall outside the breakfast-room, where he was listening, and we'd hear the whole show. Sometimes, if we laughed too loud, he would get an inkling that we were there, but by the time he had clattered noisily to his feet (deaf people can never hear the noise they are making) we were snugly back in bed, pretending to be fast asleep.

Eventually Ted Ray decided to change the format of his show, and it came to an end. It was sad, but it was time for everybody to move on.

'Variety Playhouse' with Vic Oliver was another radio programme that my mother could be heard in at around that time. She took part in little comedy sketches with Vic Oliver himself, or with Cicely Courtneidge and Jack Hulbert, in a spot that they had in the programme. Having noticed that the sketches she did with Vic Oliver were extremely well written, Patricia asked him who wrote them – and was told that it was a young writer called Johnny Speight.

'They were marvellous,' she says, 'absolutely marvellous. He wrote so well for women. In those days it was difficult to get any decent material for women. Years later, when I came to be in 'Till Death Us Do Part' I got to know Johnny Speight, and I've been his greatest admirer ever since. In fact,

when I'm asked to do a comedy series now, I say, "Well – yes
– if it's written by Johnny Speight, or someone better" – if
there is anyone better! There's always scope for good actors,
as well as comedians, in his material.'

It had been decided that, after five years of post-war
austerity, there should be held an exhibition which would
coincide with the centenary of the Great Exhibition of 1851;
and on 3 May 1951, King George VI, from the steps of St
Paul's Cathedral, declared the Festival of Britain open. The
Royal Festival Hall was built for the Festival, located on
derelict land in Lambeth on the south of the Thames, and
from this has grown the Great South Bank Complex.

Memorable features of the Festival were the Dome of
Discovery, designed by Ralph Tubbs, ornamental fountains
and the tower of a former lead-shot factory which included a
sculpture burlesque by John Piper. The Skylon, designed by
J.H. Moya, was an elegant, slender, illuminated obelisk,
which seemed to stand on its own, hence the fashionable joke
that, like Britain, the Skylon had no visible means of support!

As part of the Festival, Battersea Park was transformed
into a pleasure garden with a huge funfair, a beautifully lit
tree walk, more fountains and a grotto. The charming little
Riverside Theatre was built, and in it Leonard Sachs was
asked to present an Old Time Music Hall. The show was to
run for a month, and Leonard asked my mother to take part.
She was delighted to accept for it was a long time since she
and Leonard had worked together. Leonard was the
chairman, and my mother performed a duet with an actor
called Bill Owen – 'Three Pots a Shilling' – and an old
favourite called 'Please Sell No More Drink To My Father.'

To us, as children, the whole Festival seemed like magic; we
had never seen anything so exciting or glamorous – we were
even allowed to watch our mother perform at the Riverside
Theatre. But being children the part of the Festival that excited
us most was the Battersea funfair with its enormous big
dipper, the 'caterpillar' ride (on which there was to be a
horrific accident a few years later), the 'rota', and the best

dodgem cars. How thrilled we were to discover that the funfair was not to be taken down with the rest of the Festival in the October of that year, but was to remain in Battersea Park and be open from Easter to September each year.

9

The Comedians

During the 1950s and 1960s my mother appeared on television with nearly all the major British comedians of the period: Arthur Askey, Alfie Bass, Charlie Chester, Ken Dodd, Tony Hancock, Arthur Haynes, Benny Hill, Sid James, Hugh Lloyd, Spike Milligan, Terry Scott and Eric Sykes. It is interesting that she says that the most difficult thing for an actor to do is a light entertainment television show, with a live audience.

'They usually last about half an hour, therefore your rehearsal time is limited. If you are going to do a three-hour play, you will get three to four weeks rehearsal, two weeks for a fifty-minute play, but if you are doing a half-hour comedy show, you only get four days. In some of the Arthur Haynes shows for example, I might be in a couple of sketches – it would take me an hour to drive out to the Television Studios at Elstree, I'd rehearse for twenty minutes in one sketch, perhaps ten minutes in another short sketch, and then it would take me an hour to drive home. I would do this on Tuesday, Wednesday and Thursday, and on Friday we'd be in there doing the show. It was very nerve-racking!

'Despite this I loved working with Arthur Haynes. The scripts were brilliantly written by Johnny Speight, so that whatever part I was playing (and I usually played Arthur Haynes' wife), even if I only had five lines, they would be spot on, with a wonderful character that I could get to grips with.'

My mother has always had the highest respect for Johnny Speight, and he for her. He says:

'Working with Pat has been a real pleasure all the way through. She is like me – not very demonstrative – but you can tell when she appreciates your work. She will criticize if she has to say something that does not fit in with her character, but I cannot recall any unpleasantness. She is also marvellous company, but like me she does not socialize because she does not drink. Pat has something that has always appealed to me as a writer – a streak of madness. Irene Handl had it, Peter Sellers had it, all the great ones have it.'

'The Arthur Haynes Show' consisted of a series of sketches; in one of these Arthur played a lovable old layabout who always managed to get the better of the authorities. His straight man was Nicolas Parsons. (It is interesting to note that Nicolas Parsons is married to Denise Brier, another woman who used to play a lot of boys on the radio.) My mother remembers some amusing moments from those particular sketches, frequently caused by the fact that they had had so little rehearsal. One sketch, in which she played Arthur Haynes' wife, was set in a very smart restaurant; another couple of tramps, played by Dermot Kelly and Rita Webb, made up the party of four. The aggravated *maître d'hôtel*, Nicolas Parsons, tried to turn them out, but Arthur had booked a table. During the dialogue which followed they were all involved in ordering the food. Dermot Kelly was supposed to order 'soup with potatoes and dumplings' but during the take, because he was Irish, he decided to change the word 'potatoes' to 'spuds'. It is not a good idea to make changes during a take. Dermot said, with his lovely Irish accent, 'Just some soup with spuds and – some – uh – some – rhubarb.'

It is not difficult to imagine the reaction from the rest of the cast, who all exploded with laughter. 'Arthur was very good at keeping a straight face,' recalls my mother, 'but he was shaking. I had my back to the camera, fortunately, but my shoulders were heaving Rita Webb was whispering, "Stop it," to me; she was good at not laughing.'

Dermot Kelly, a very popular Irish character actor, was, says Johnny Speight, 'A lovely fellow, and remembering the characters he always played, it may surprise you to know that he came from a very middle-class family in Dublin. His sister was a leading journalist and his brother was a well-known lawyer.'

Arthur Haynes and Nicolas Parson worked together for several years and over the years they developed some amusing impromptu games during the show. They would suddenly interrupt one another in the middle of a sketch and start 'ad libbing', vying with each other as to who could be the funniest or go on the longest without laughing. One day they were in the middle of a sketch in which Nicolas Parsons was the Lord of the Manor and Arthur a tramp who had come to apply for the position of butler. 'This is the wife, Yvonne,' he said, pointing to my mother. 'She's a good little worker. If she's any trouble, just let me know and I'll give her a thump.' Just before this line, Arthur and Nicolas went off into one of their 'ad lib' sessions. They went on for so long and got so far away from the original script that my mother realized they were lost.

'I decided to prompt Arthur, so I turned my back to the camera, got near to him and whispered, 'Thump'. He said, 'What was that?' I repeated 'Thump', burst out laughing, lost control and wet the floor. I spent the rest of the scene standing over the little wet patch, hoping that nobody had noticed it. I thought I was helping Arthur because he had dried. He twisted it round to his own advantage. I learned never to do that again.'

The musical spot in 'The Arthur Haynes Show' was always filled by a well-known singer or group. My mother met many people: Lulu, Gerry and the Pacemakers, Freddie and the Dreamers, Sandie Shaw, Adam Faith. My sister Gemma was absolutely thrilled; she would go to the rehearsals with my mother and meet all her heart-throbs.

Athur Haynes died suddenly from heart failure in 1966; he was only fifty-two.

The Ken Dodd shows were of a completely different format, always based on Variety. Ken Dodd has a very pleasant singing voice; he would tell jokes and stories, sing a song or two on his own, and perform routines with his lovely little 'Diddy Men'. Amongst all the Variety, there would be some sketches. My mother remembers: 'I was sent for one day to be in one of Ken Dodd's shows. I had to go up to Manchester with the Scottish actor John Laurie. When we arrived that night we went to meet Ken Dodd, and he introduced us to his scriptwriter Eddie Braben.'

This was the start of a long relationship with Ken Dodd and Eddie Braben. Ken Dodd was always extremely generous to my mother; he liked her work and appreciated her and was one of the few comics who would stand back and laugh as she was rehearsing. Eddie Braben was a very clever writer.

'Once Eddie Braben cottoned on to the fact that I could do rather straight dramatic roles,' says my mother, 'he started to write "cod dramatic" sketches. I had lots of lovely unusual snippets of things to do. Ken Dodd really enjoyed it and lured me on to be more and more dramatic and over the top.

'However, the Ken Dodd shows had their hair-raising moments. The main reason was that Ken and Eddie were always having new and better ideas, not only during the rehearsals but during the actual take. They would keep handing us other little sketches. We would be told that if there was time we would be doing this sketch and that, playing this part and that. I think they thought, "There are only two or three lines, they'll just read it through and they'll know it." The result was that the take would go on for hours. The shows had a live audience; but they did not go out live. They were edited afterwards before being televised.

'In order to save money, because the musicians in the orchestra would be paid for any overtime worked, we would have to start the take by recording the orchestral introduction and parade, followed immediately by the orchestral play-out and finale. Then the orchestra would be allowed to go home, and we would record the show itself. Eventually the producer would come downstairs telling Ken that he had to finish. Ken was absolutely tireless and would have gone on all night.'

One day my mother said to Rita Webb, who was also in the show, 'Oh, Rita, I'm so nervous. Not only have I got to remember all the things that we've rehearsed, but suppose he finds time to slip in even more? I'll never learn this little speech!'

Rita Webb replied, 'Don't worry, Pat, don't worry. Say a prayer – now I always say a little prayer before the show. Kneel down.' So she knelt down. 'Put your hands together, and I'll say the prayer for both of us. Dear God – please help Pat and me get through the show. Please don't let us forget our lines and please don't let us "Fluff"!'

Actors call it a 'fluff' when they make mistakes on individual words during a take. One actor my mother knew, who was particularly nervous about broadcasting, said that he thought he could make a fortune by walking up and down the street outside Broadcasting House, selling 'anti-fluff pills'.

Recording the finale of the show before the rest of the take sometimes caused considerable confusion. There was an occasion when Judith Chalmers, who was always in Ken Dodd's radio show, appeared in one of the television sketches. The finale was recorded before the actual programme; and when the programme went out Judith's sketch had been cut – yet there she was, in the finale. It must have been very bewildering for the viewers.

It was in that same show that my mother relates: 'When I was made-up and ready and came down to do the opening number, I discovered eight beautiful model girls wearing those very revealing cut-away costumes, all sparkling, with feathered tails and plumed head-dresses. With the girls were eight absolutely gorgeous Afghan hounds, bored out of their minds, waiting, waiting, waiting. When I asked what was happening with the dogs, I was told that during the opening parade the girls were going to walk around the stage, each one leading one of the gorgeous dogs. I went out front to watch that part of the opening. There they were on the stage, free at last to move. Their long coats were rippling and they were beautifully lit. When the programme eventually came out, all you saw were the tops of the girls; their arms were stretched out as if they were attached to something, which must have been the dogs' leads, but there was no sign of the dogs at all. They were out of shot. What a waste of those beautiful creatures.'

Working with Tony Hancock was fascinating, but a very different experience. My mother had been in some of his radio shows and was eventually asked to be in 'Hancock's Half Hour' on Television. The shows were brilliantly written by Ray Galton and Alan Simpson, who later went on to write 'Steptoe and Son'.

Galton and Simpson met at the age of 17 in a sanatorium, where they were recovering from tuberculosis, and started writing for the entertainments put on in the sanatorium. Eventually they wrote to Frank Muir and Dennis Norden, asking them how they could become professional script-writers. Frank Muir and Dennis Norden replied, telling them to send any ideas for a script to the BBC. As soon as they came out of the sanatorium this was what they did.

At first my mother was not a regular part of 'Hancock's Half Hour'; however one day Duncan Wood, who directed the shows, came to her and said, 'A great honour is going to be bestowed on you. You are going to play Mrs Crevatte, the charwoman, who has so far never been seen but only talked about.'

Galton and Simpson remember: 'She was lovely as Mrs Crevatte. She was Hancock's landlady, but it was also her job to clean his room and get his breakfast. She used to do it with such bad grace, virtually slinging his breakfast at him. Her behaviour was rude and totally disrespectful, treating Hancock with complete contempt. The character Hancock played wanted respect from his menials; if he was paying somebody 2s 6d per hour to "do for him", he wanted to be treated like the Squire of the Manor. Whereas to Mrs Crevatte he was just a layabout, out-of-work actor.

'The thing we always found it difficult to reconcile with Pat, was that she was always so well spoken when she was off, difficult to imagine as that terrible cockney woman that she played. She is so genteel as a person, and so coarse as many of the characters she plays.'

My mother described the character of Mrs Crevatte as 'outrageous, discontented and moody'. She had some wonderful scenes, such as that in the now legendary 'The Cold', in which she endeavours to cure Tony Hancock of a very bad head cold by means of voodoo, waving her arms around and chanting:

> 'Ague, Ague, hear me shout
> Ague, Ague, come on out!'

When Hancock realized that it was Mrs Crevatte who was coming to cure him, he said to Sid James: 'No, get her out of here. I'm not letting her have anything to do with me. I'll be dead of pneumonia by the time she's finished with me.'

The most memorable thing about Mrs Crevatte visually was her hat, which was cited in a Sunday paper as one of the six funniest things on television that particular year.

Tony Hancock himself was quiet and morose. Apparently he hardly spoke to my mother at all during the time that she was working with him. She says, 'I found it difficult to understand why he was so morbid, because to me he seemed to have everything. He was enormously in demand and very successful. On top of that he was unusually gifted.'

There were a few times when the normally sour Hancock would have to laugh like anybody else. Galton and Simpson recall, 'When Hancock used to break up and laugh, he would cry with laughter and he just couldn't stop. There was one occasion in the very early days. We were working a radio show called 'Calling All Forces'. Charlie Chester and Tony Hancock were the regulars and each week there were guest artists; that particular week the guest artist was Bernard Braden. The story was set in Canada, near Hudson Bay, and it was a sort of Whitehall farce with people going in and out of doors in igloos. At the first read-through something caught Hancock's imagination and he started laughing. Well, he laughed and laughed – in the end he fell off his chair and was just rolling about on the floor. It took him about five minutes to recover. He was a sombre man but there were many occasions when he 'went' during the live radio shows, though very seldom on the television show because he was so strung-up. Speaking from memory, the only time that it happened during a television show, Dick Emery was in it. Tony had bought a house off Sid James during the fog. He moved in, but when the fog lifted he found it was on the runway at Heathrow Airport. Every time a plane went over the whole house used to shake. Hancock was trying to re-sell the house to a young couple played by Dick Emery and an actress, and was wandering round the house showing it to them. What was supposed to happen was that a plane took off and the house started to shake and one by one the things collapsed and finally the fireplace was meant to crash to the ground. However the plane did not go over, but things started to fall down, and the fireplace fell down five minutes before it was supposed to. The show was going out live, so Hancock had to hold the fireplace up instead of showing them around the house, shouting his lines to them from the living room. He was beside himself with laughter, and so were the audience, and when the plane finally flew over he turned to the camera and said, "surprise, surprise!" '

According to Galton and Simpson, Hancock and my mother had one amazing quality in common. They were both brilliant sight-readers. Many actors stumble and stutter when they are first handed the script to read. 'When Pat and Hancock used to rehearse together at the first read-through it was as if they both knew it by heart. Immaculate. Every inflection would be perfect, all the timing would be right. It was just an instinct with both of them. If Pat had been a man she would have been a big star years ago! We often tried to book her for our other shows, and we wanted her to play the part of one of the family in "Steptoe", but she was always so busy.'

There came a time when my mother was asked to do another series of 'Hancock's Half Hour', and her agent requested a pay rise. The request was not granted; and, what was more, somebody else was hired. However, she was asked back for the next series, and Tony Hancock said to her, 'The trouble with you is that you are too expensive.'

'Well, Tony,' said my mother bravely, 'I think I'm worth about half of what you get.'

'No, you are not,' said Tony. 'When you're as well known as I am, then, you'll be worth about half what I get!'

'No – when I'm as well known as you are, I'll be worth the same as you are.' Whereupon Tony Hancock walked out of the room.

The other actor, already mentioned, who was always with Tony Hancock in those early programmes was the unforgettable Sid James. It is difficult to understand why Hancock suddenly dropped him. He was perfectly happy to play second fiddle to Hancock, and apparently he was really nervous of fronting his own show when Hancock ditched him. Galton and Simpson told me that they wrote the show 'Citizen James' for him as compensation for not doing any more 'Hancock's'. Sid was as charming and easy to get on with as Tony was difficult. He was always greatly loved and respected by his fellow actors, and it was a very sad loss to the profession when he died so suddenly in 1976.

Some time after my mother had been in her last 'Hancock's Half Hour', she was contacted by producer Ken Carter, who said, 'I'm doing some advertisements with Tony Hancock for the Egg Marketing Board. They have a slogan every year and this year the slogan is going to be "Happiness is Egg-shaped". Now we are all set and ready to do them tomorrow, but last night I had a session with Tony and he said that he refuses to say 'Happiness is Egg-shaped'. I went back to the sponsors and they insist that he says it, because the whole campaign is based on the slogan. Tony still refuses to say it. Eventually I pointed out to Tony that he could lose thousands of pounds and that the Egg Marketing Board might well sue him; and then I suggested that someone else might say the line, someone like Patricia Hayes as Mrs Crevatte. All that he would have to do would be to react to the line. He has agreed. Now, are you available?'

She *was* available, and that was how she came to be in a very funny series of promotions for the Egg Marketing Board. Strangely enough, when they went to the BBC wardrobe to get the Mrs Crevatte hat, it had completely disappeared. In desperation my mother made up a hat herself from our dressing-up box, and decorated it with fruit and flowers.

'Hugh and I' was another successful situation comedy of the 1960s, co-starring Terry Scott and Hugh Lloyd, and written by John Chapman. My mother was employed for two thirteen-week series, and thoroughly enjoyed them. Terry Scott and Hugh Lloyd were very warm and charming to her. She says, however, that the series was made for her by Cyril Smith, who played her husband.

'I'd never met him before, but the day we all arrived for the first read-through an elderly man came up to me and said; "Good morning, Patricia, I am Cyril Smith and I'm going to play your husband, Mr Wormold. I thought I'd like to take the opportunity at the same time to bring you a copy of the script of the new *Sailor, Beware* play that is going to be done. If you like the part, I am going to suggest to the management that you play the role that Esma Cannon used to do, because she does not want to do it any more. She has gone to live abroad with her husband, and you would be absolutely perfect.'

From that moment onwards they went on to become the greatest colleagues, and she did play the Esma Cannon part in *Rock-a-bye Sailor*. More of that later. Cyril Smith and my mother became very popular as the funny little neighbours, the Wormolds, in 'Hugh and I'. They loved one another's company, and would regale each other with wonderful tales of their careers. My mother had no one to talk to about her career except her children – not that we weren't interested, but we weren't adult – and although Cyril Smith was happily married, his wife was not interested in all the gossip from the business; and my mother is an extremely good listener and laughed at all his jokes. Sadly, Cyril Smith died and had to be replaced in 'Hugh and I'. The other actors in the cast were Violet Stevens, Molly Sugden and Wallace Eaton.

Rock-a-bye Sailor was fraught with problems from the very beginning. *Sailor, Beware* was the first of the trio of plays written by Philip King and Falkland Cary, followed by *Watch it, Sailor*. The central character in all the plays is a very robust but ultimately vulnerable dragon of a woman, Emma Hornet, originally played by Peggy Mount, who was superb. Kathleen Harrison, a fine English comedy actress, played Emma in *Watch it, Sailor* and was very good although not as ideal for the part. Renee Houston, a Scottish comedienne, was finally cast as Emma Hornet in *Rock-a-bye Sailor*. But, from the beginning, she was never right for the part. The character is profoundly cockney, and Renee is Scottish; secondly, Renee was essentially a comedienne, used to performing in the halls and unused to the rigorous disciplines of the straight theatre. She never really knew her lines, or thought it was particularly necessary to learn them. She complained to my mother one day, because she had been called in for extra rehearsals since it was considered that she did not know the lines, 'Look, Flower, I've been in the business for fifty years, and I've never been short of something to say on stage!' All the other actors would take their scripts home after the rehearsals, to go through them ready for the next day while Renee would just leave her script on the set.

Unfortunately, since the central character is always so important in a play, *Rock-a-bye Sailor* was a flop, which was a great pity because, according to my mother, the play itself was probably the funniest of the trio.

Charlie Chester had his own television series based on an Edgar Wallace character, called 'Educated Evans'. He was a wise wide-boy of the Edwardian era. My mother played his sister-in-law, Emma Toggs, who had it in for him; he was the hero, and her character was funny but nasty. She does not remember a lot about the series, except that it was enjoyable, and that Charlie Chester was good to work with. However, one incident remains in her mind. Apparently she said to a fellow actor, 'Isn't it wonderful to think that we've got thirteen weeks' work with this series?'

'Yes,' he replied, 'its nice to have thirteen weeks' work – but sometimes I think it's quite good to be out of work, too. I'll tell you why. When you are in work, you know what you are going to be doing for thirteen weeks, we know more or less what we will be doing every day. When you are out of work anything can happen. The phone can ring and tomorrow you will be on a plane to America.'

'You have the perfect temperament to be an actor,' said my mother. 'That's what you need – an adventurous spirit. Or to be able to live at home, as I did when I was a struggling young actress.'

Arthur Askey also had his own television series, 'Arthur's Treasured Volumes', which went out on ATV (the same initials!) The marvellous June Whitfield played Arthur's wife and my mother played a neighbour 'married' to Arthur Mullard. The programme was directed by Josephine Douglas, who was also responsible for Six-Five Special, television's first teenage pop music show.

My mother was also in some episodes of 'Bootsie and Snudge', with Alfie Bass and Bill Fraser and an occasional 'Sykes' with Eric Sykes and Hattie Jacques. She loved all the comedians, and always spoke of them in glowing terms, but when forced to tell who was her favourite she said, 'Benny Hill. Not only because he gave me the most marvellous opportunities in his shows, but because he released me from my contract to let me play *Edna the Inebriate Woman*.'

My mother worked a great deal with Benny Hill, both on radio and on television. Benny Hill's writer was Dave Freeman, who was also an actor. He wrote some marvellous parts for my mother, and Benny Hill gave her some terrific opportunities. There was, of course, the Edie Grimthorpe character, who always turned up like a bad penny. Benny would meet a gorgeous female, he would ask her out and she would insist on bringing her friend, called Edie Grimthorpe, played by my mother. In order to make up a foursome Benny would bring a mate along. The mate was always completely gormless. Inevitably the gorgeous girl would wander off into the moonlight with Benny's gormless mate, and he would be left with my mother, who would say, 'Ooh, you are artful, the way you got rid of them two, so we could be on our own together,' giving Benny the opportunity to look straight into camera and say, 'Big deal!'

Edie Grimthorpe cropped up again and again, and my mother commented on it, 'Oh, it's Edie Grimthorpe again. She always turns up, and you always get lumbered.'

'Yes,' replied Benny. 'It's the story of my life.'

She once said to him, regarding a particular group of comedians, 'They are all married except you. Why haven't you got married?'

'I've been waiting for you, haven't I? Waiting for you to be free.'

'Well, I am free now,' my mother told him.

'Oh God!' was Benny Hill's reply.

Sometimes my mother played the gorgeous woman, a man-eating vamp made up to look like Zsa Zsa Gabor, who managed to lure Benny into her clutches and imprison him in her apartment. On one occasion she was supposed to drive past Benny Hill in a very glamorous car, and try to pick him up. Burnham Beeches was chosen as a location, and a magnificent car obtained for her. However, when she got into the car, there was absolutely no way that she could reach the pedals. 'They had to give the car a push, so that I went sailing along as though I was driving! They could not start the engine because my feet were so far away from the pedals. I had to look as if I was sitting back on the seat with great long legs. Even with the seat as far forward as it would go, there was no way that I could have driven the car.'

Dave Freeman wrote various different types of sketches for Benny. There were some which were built around certain well established characters: the old man, the commissionaire, the Chinaman with the false teeth. These were all masterpieces of writing for Benny. Then there were the 'take-offs' – for example a skit based on Ken Russell's famous television film about Delius. Benny was Delius, the old blind musician, (played in the film by Max Adrian) and my mother was the patient wife, based on Maureen Prior's characterization in the film. One of the funniest and cleverest sketches was the parody of the film *The Knack*, with Benny as the Michael Crawford character and my mother as Rita Tushingham. It was hilarious to see her looking so trendy in the mini-skirted black and white outfits based on Mary Quant's fashions of the period. These cod-movies were usually speeded up and deliberately very badly cut, with no continuity. Benny would be seen leaving the room wearing one outfit but in the external shot showing him coming out of that same room he would be wearing something slightly different.

Benny Hill was great fun to work with every day, until it came to the day of the take. According to my mother, on that day he underwent a personality change. Once she accused him, saying, 'You are absolutely wonderful until the day of the show, then you have a complete change of personality.'

The reason was that, on that day, the responsibility of the show fell well and truly on his shoulders. There was no question of laughing about anything, it had to be right. Apart from all the sketches, he had all the musical numbers, long songs with complicated words, as well as constant changes of costume and make-up and the different sets and scenes. It must have been exhausting.

However, as with all television comedy shows, there was too little rehearsal time, and sometimes it was extremely difficult to be controlled when things went wrong. Although my mother did occasionally laugh, most of the time she found enormous strength to resist the temptation. She says that one of the reasons for this goes back to 1938. 'One of the things that I detest is laughing on stage in the middle of a performance. It is so unprofessional. When Frank Pettingell (who was absolutely marvellous as the eccentric photographer) became bored during *When We Are Married*, he set out to try and make me laugh. Night after night he would think of something. In the end I thought to myself, nothing that he does is going to make me laugh. Eventually it did not matter what he did, it was not funny as far as I was concerned.'

There is one particular sketch that Benny Hill always teases my mother over. He says, 'You ruined that sketch by laughing!' But my mother says, 'In fact he knows that it is not true. What really happened was that *he* ruined the sketch by laughing.' Benny, in the character of Jolly the Jokemonger, sells a woman (my mother) a mask that looks like a wolf's head, for her little boy. The outcome is that the boy gets the mask wedged firmly on his head and the woman returns to the shop, angrily dragging the boy with her, to complain to Jolly the Jokemonger. The mask that they were using was very hot, and the boy was told not to wear it at the rehearsals. Consequently no one had seen him in the wolf's head mask until the actual take. As soon as Benny saw the boy, he was convulsed with laughter and could hardly manage to say his line, something to the effect of: 'He looks nice, it suits him.'

During one of the Benny Hill shows my mother said to Benny, quite innocently, 'I had to turn down a television play the other day because of these shows.'

Benny Hill said, straight away, 'You should not have done that. You should have got on the phone to me and told me that you had been offered a play, and I would have released you.'

When the enquiry came as to my mother's availability to play *Edna, The Inebriate Woman*, my mother was committed to four Benny Hill shows for Thames Television. However, she told Hazel de Leon not to turn it down. Remembering what Benny Hill had said, she asked Hazel to contact Philip Jones (Head of Light Entertainment at Thames Television). Shortly afterwards word came through that Benny would be prepared to release her.

'Benny was always extremely loyal to the people who worked with him,' my mother says. 'Maybe it gave him a get-out, too, and a chance to use some new blood in the show.'

During the speech my mother made when she accepted her award for her performance in *Edna the Inebriate Woman*, she said, 'I could not have won this award if it had not been for Benny Hill, who released me from a contract.' As she said it, she could see him smiling from his table, and she hoped he was not thinking, 'Little does she know I was glad to get rid of her!'

Although she was so busy and in demand during those years, she still maintained all her family responsibilities. We each passed the eleven-plus examination, and went off to a grammar school. I was sent to boarding school, because my mother had always wanted to go to one herself, to Combe Bank, Convent of the Holy Child, near Westerham in Kent. Gemma went off to Our Lady of Sion Convent, in Notting Hill Gate, and Richard to Wimbledon College, the Jesuit school where Brian had been educated.

At a time when it was still quite unusual to own a car, Richard arrived home one day to find his mother pointing to a receipt for a Morris Series 3, price £550. 'You haven't bought a car, have you?', he asked. She nodded and he burst into tears of joy! His love of cars and motor bikes developed at an early age, and by the time he was nineteen he had owned several bikes, and then bought an old taxi. Richard and his friends used to pile into the taxi with me and as many of my more attractive girlfriends as I could muster. We would crawl slowly all the way to Brighton with the rest of the traffic on Bank Holidays. Poor Richard – he suffered the burden of all older brothers: I was allowed to go out as long as I was 'with Richard'. At all the parties and school dances I would be tagging along. When we left school, Richard pursued a course in motor vehicle technology, I went to the Guildhall School of Music and Drama to have my voice trained, and Gemma took an arts degree at Warwick University.

10

Film Making in Malta
to the Making of *Edna*

Hazel de Leon rang my mother one day: 'Patricia, dear –
Antony Newley wants to see you at his offices in Park Lane.
He is making a film, and is interested in you for the part of
his mother. It will mean three months in Malta.'

Antony Newley stared at my mother for a long time
during the interview. Then came the routine questions about
her background, after which he asked, 'What's your birth
date?' When she replied that it was 22 December, he said,
'Oh, yes, you are on the cusp of Sagittarius and Capricorn.'
Somehow that seemed to confirm his decision: she looked
right, her experience was broad and relevant, and, in
conjunction with these factors, her stars were favourable. The
part was hers.

The film had the unbelievable title of *Can Hieronymus
Merkin Ever Forget Mercy Humppe and Find True
Happiness?* It was written by Antony Newley and Hermann
Raucher, with music by Antony Newley, starred Antony
Newley and was produced and directed by Antony Newley!
To say that it was partially autobiographical would be an
understatement; Joan Collins, to whom he was then married,
even played his wife and both his children were in the movie
too. It was the story of a Hollywood film idol recapturing his

past life and fantasies through a film-within-a-film that he is screening for his children at the seaside.

One at a time the stars from England and America came and went, Stubby Kaye, Bruce Forsyth, Judy Cornwall, Victor Spinetti. The longest stay for them would be perhaps ten days, but the character of the mother kept recurring all through Hieronymus Merkin's life and, as they were not going to do the 'reverse shots' until the end of the shoot, my mother had to be in Malta for the whole of the summer. It was one of the best summers she has ever had. She moved out of her hotel after the first four days. She has never enjoyed hotel living: 'I could not stand it. It was all luxury – but food I could not eat and water I could not drink. Tea you could not bear the taste of, because it was all made from desalinated water. Eventually I discovered that if you went right up to Mdina, the ancient capital of Malta, there were wells. I used to go to the Convent of the Sacred Heart and come staggering out with a crate full of bottles, not of wine or whisky, but of well water which was drinkable and which made a decent cup of tea. I moved into an apartment in a block of four; the other apartments were inhabited by members of the film crew, who were also there for the whole summer and were very friendly. Mine was the ground-floor flat, with a pretty little balcony overlooking the beach, although it was not very 'ground' because there was a flight of steps leading up into the building. I was able to do all my own catering, which I always prefer. I hired a car and ventured out into the treacherous Maltese traffic. The motorists there felt no necessity to drive on a particular side of the road; at a moment's notice, if it suited them, they would change to the other side!'

My mother got on very well with Antony Newley and Joan Collins, both of whom she admired enormously. Joan Collins was very professional. Recently, after she'd become so famous in soap operas, a director who was about to work with her said to my mother, 'I'm terrified of working with Joan Collins.' My mother quickly responded, 'You don't have to be. Nobody is more professional than she is. She doesn't mess about, and she is easy to direct.'

Later the director came back to my mother: 'How right you were about Joan Collins.'

'Yes,' said my mother. 'People think that she is like the character that she is playing. She is not like that at all. She is very, very down to earth, and a kind and loving mother.'

However, one day someone said to Joan Collins, within my mother's earshot, 'Aren't you lucky to be married to Tony Newley? He is so gifted, he sings, he acts, he directs.'

'Yes, I suppose so,' Joan said, 'but we haven't got a thing in common.' My mother felt that perhaps Joan was more down to earth than Tony.

One of the things my mother liked about Tony Newley was that, physically, he was at ease with everybody. He was very tactile, but not in a way that anyone could take offence to. He would often put his arms around the cameramen or one of the crew while he was explaining exactly what he wanted in a certain shot. His children would be climbing all over him as he was directing the film. They were the only people who were allowed to interrupt when he was busy.

The role my mother was playing was not taxing; very often she would be in shot with nothing to say. There were many days when she was not needed at all, so she was able to relax into the longest paid holiday of a lifetime. The weather was wonderful, nearly always warm and sunny. The scenery was dramatic, rocky and dry. She used to drive to some of the favourite beaches to swim. Some of our friends took the opportunity of joining her there for no more than the cost of their airfares. When she returned she was browner and more relaxed than I have ever seen her. We were all invited out for part of the summer; I was restricted, with small children, and Richard and Gemma were working. (Gemma did, however, find time to squeeze in a marriage ceremony, and startled our mother by sending her a telegram with little more than the date – 3·5·68 – and the dramatic single word – 'Married').

The Beatles had rocketed to fame and stardom during the

1960s and my mother had worked with the fabulous four in their film *Help!*, released in 1965. There was very little opportunity of speaking to the Liverpool heroes, because they were extremely busy but my mother found them pleasant and natural. She played a very small part as an Eastern woman, all blacked up and swathed in a sari. Her scene involved a beautiful Indian girl who was naked in a bath. Those were the days when body painting was all the rage, and the young girl's body was painted with an exotic pattern from the waist upwards. Before they started shooting the young girl confided to my mother, 'I'm terribly worried, they said to me that I had to be in a bath, but I did not realize that I would have no clothes on. I need the money but my husband would be furious if he thought that people were going to see me without my clothes!' Poor girl. At least no one was allowed in to watch the take, even the Beatles themselves, although – according to my mother – it was not for want of trying; they even scaled the scenery flats.

Barry Took, one of England's best-loved humorists, and actor John Junkin came up with a fascinating idea towards the end of the 1960s. It was well ahead of its time. They adapted the extraordinary characters from J.B. Morton's 'Beachcomber' column in the *Daily Express* (a column so popular that many people would buy the paper just to read it) and brought them to life for television. Duncan Wood directed the series and he chose Spike Milligan to hold the programme together in the character of Dr Strabismus – and what an extraordinary performance he gave, completely zany! The set was brilliant, too, a sort of forerunner of the set for *Cats* – not back-alley rubbish, but high-class people's junk, old broken antiques, desks, lamps, books, a telescope and a huge globe. There were many marvellous parts, and Duncan Wood surrounded himself with a wealth of comedy talent. Sheila Steafel, a very clever comedienne, Frank Thornton, one of our best comedy actors, later to become famous as Captain Peacock in 'Are You Being Served', Clive

Dunn, who has perfected a speciality of playing rickety old men, such as Mr Jones, the excitable butcher in 'Dad's Army', Julian Orchard, a brilliant comedy actor who died tragically young a few years later, just as his career was taking off, Hattie Jacques, exotic and rotund, most remembered for the role of Eric Sykes' eccentric and long-suffering sister in 'Sykes', Sir Michael Redgrave, who each week stood very seriously in a huge hall, behind a solemn lectern, and read from a list of Huntingdonshire cabmen. One name I remember was Mousecarpet! There were thirteen real, red-bearded dwarfs and last, but by no means least, the extremely versatile Patricia Hayes.

Amongst the caricatures that my mother played, the one that she enjoyed the most was Mrs McGurgle, the 'refeened' Blackpool landlady. Her experiences with real Blackpool landladies during the war gave her tremendous insight into the part. She wore a grotesque red wig, false eyelashes and brightly coloured 'mutton-dressed-as-lamb' outfits. Her accent was that of a working-class Northerner, desperately giving herself airs and graces, which distorted all her vowel sounds. Her attitudes were narrow-minded and self-opinionated. It was extremely funny. However, she says, 'It was wonderful to do such meaty material, and very difficult not to laugh when the audience laughed. I was so nervous, not because I was afraid of forgetting the lines but because I was terrified I would laugh when I was being funny. It was my biggest undertaking to date, creative, off-beat humour. I wish they would repeat it; it would stand the test of time, it really would.'

Joy Whitby, who was originally a BBC producer and director, and who started the very popular children's programme 'Jackanory', went over to ITV at its inception. However, the politics within the new television company caused some resignations and Joy Whitby was among those who resigned. Finding herself out of a job, she set to work to make a screenplay out of a story she had invented. It became a thirteen-episode serial for children's television, 'Grasshop-per Island'. It was a delightful story written around her three sons, aged fifteen, eleven and seven. They went off on an adventure, which took them to an island where they met a strange professor and his housekeeper. The children were in search of hidden treasure, and the professor was searching for a blue grasshopper. The location for the shoot was the island of Corsica, Napoleon's birthplace. Joy Whitby managed to hire Tony Leggo, one of England's best television cameramen to do the camera work, a friend of hers, Doreen Stephens, produced it and she directed it herself. Julian Orchard played the professor and my mother his housekeeper. Once again she had a wonderful stay, though only two and a half weeks this time. They filmed all over Corsica, on the beaches where the sea was the brilliant blue characteristic of the Mediterranean, in the vineyards and in the countryside among the dry-leaved olive trees. At night most of the small cast ate together, absorbing the harsh but comforting sounds of the crickets.

After her return home, my mother resumed work in another series of 'The Benny Hill Show'. It was during this series that Hazel contacted her: 'A lovely part for you has come along, Patricia. I don't know if you will want to do it because she is a drinker – an alcoholic.' (My mother has always been a non-drinker.) 'The play has been written by Jeremy Sandford, and is called *Edna the Inebriate Woman*. Do you think they will release you from the Benny Hill shows?'

Good fortune and timing, life's all-important ingredients, came together for my mother on this occasion. Kathleen Harrison was first offered the part, but she turned it down under the advice of her family. She had been very ill; many of the scenes during *Edna* were to be filmed outside at night, and the weather was very cold. Her bad luck became my mother's good luck, and Kathleen Harrison wished her well. She was only too aware of the fact that this was an award-winning role.

My mother says, 'I read the script and, as I read it, I could not believe that I was being given first refusal. It was the sort of part that every actor dreams of, a once in a lifetime opportunity that could lead anywhere. I said yes at once. Jeremy Sandford, the author, is an ingenious writer deeply committed to exposing social injustices such as the plight of outcasts in our affluent society. He was already famous for writing the screenplay of "Cathy Come Home", the tragic story of a homeless mother. The director was to be a Canadian, Ted Kotchev. That night I happened to be working in a charity performance with an actor called Paul Curran. He enquired what I was doing; I mentioned *Edna* and he asked me who was to direct. When I told him it was Ted Kotchev there was a pause, and then he said "You lucky, lucky woman." I asked why, and he said, "Well, all I can say is that Ted Kotchev is a human dynamo. He's like the sun, when he shines on you – you blossom. He is the most marvellous director that I have ever worked with." Those words proved to be absolutely true for me.'

Ted Kotchev rang my mother almost immediately after she had accepted the role, and arranged to visit her that day because the filming was to start any day. He wanted to have a long chat with her about the character of Edna, take her to see The Shelter (a home for down-and-outs in Lambeth) and round the day off by taking her out to dinner, as is the custom for a director and his leading lady.

'We discussed Edna in great detail; it was tremendous to discover that we were in complete agreement about the character of this brave, tragic and frequently outrageous individual. I was deeply flattered when he revealed that, once my name had been suggested for the role of Edna, he would not consider anybody else. He would have waited for me, if I had not been available straight away. He then suggested a trip to this house called The Shelter in Lambeth. This was to be the model for the home that Edna finally gets into, called "Jesus Saves", and from whence they were so cruelly evicted when she thought that she had at last found a permanent place to stay. Ted drove me to The Shelter, and we met the woman who ran it. It was the first glimpse I had had of how these down-and-out women really live. The house is basically run by the wives of wealthy men who are involved in charity work. Downstairs there was a kitchen where there were always some basic groceries, eggs, bacon, bread and some cheap crockery and utensils. Apparently the women came in daily and helped themselves to food, though not one of them ever did any cleaning or clearing, not even the washing-up! They resent having to do anything, but they accept the charity, feeling that they are entitled to it. Upstairs there were rooms with truckle beds, but no wardrobes. When I asked where they kept their clothes I was told, "It's no good having wardrobes, because they keep their bundle of things under their beds. This plastic bundle is not to be touched by anybody else, it is their personal private property. Occasionally they wash out a few things but they never throw anything away."

'When we finally came outside again it was quite cold and Ted asked me where I would like to go and eat. I said to him, "To go out and eat would be, as far as I'm concerned, a complete waste of money. You can come back with me if you like, and I'll cook you something, or you can just drop me at home. I'm really too tired to enjoy a big meal, I've got nervous exhaustion with all the excitement." He said, "Great – I'll take you home and then I'll go back and spend the evening with my wife, she sees so little of me." With that he dropped me at my house, and off he went. I could tell he was thankful, because he was tired too, but he was prepared to do the right thing and entertain me.'

The next day she was taken to the BBC Wardrobe where she was looked after by Barbara Nixon. Between them they decided what Edna looked like, and my mother chose the distinctive hat. Two days later they started filming, with only a month in hand.

The play was called *Edna the Inebriate Woman*, so on the very first day they started shooting, on her very first line, my mother spoke with a slightly slurred pronunciation. Ted Kotchev's reaction was immediate. 'Patricia – don't be drunk.'

'Not in this scene?'

'Not in any scene.'

'But she is called the Inebriate Woman.' She had imagined that she was going to play an old drunk wandering through the script.

'OK, she's called the Inebriate Woman – but you play this as a drunk, and after five minutes every television set in the country will be switched off, because drunks are bores! There are just two places where you can be drunk. She is not an alcoholic, Edna, they call her the Inebriate Woman because in desperation, from time to time, she will drink anything to console herself for the agony life is to her. She will just go out and pour a whole bottle of meths down her throat. Then she'll be blind drunk. Basically, if she were happy, she wouldn't be bothering to drink at all.' Many a lesser director would have realized too late that playing all the scenes blind drunk would have become tiresome and boring.

Ted Kotchev was a perfectionist who wanted only the best, consequently he had surrounded himself with a top-quality cast and crew. The cameramen, sound technicians, designers, make-up artists were all second to none. From the moment she met Ted Kotchev, my mother realized that she was going to be working with a genius, although she says that she never got to know Ted Kotchev, the man. 'We never had time for personal conversations – but he was an extremely inspiring director. His powers of concentration were amazing; whatever you did, you had his full concentration. He was like the perfect audience, which in a way is what a director should be, a perfect audience and a perfect critic. He did not need to show me what to do; he would say, for example, "You should be making me very sad, and you're not," or "I feel you are trying to be funny but you are not really funny." '

When a scene was going well, no one was more ready with praise than Ted Kotchev, nobody laughed louder than he did;

he had an eagle eye and noticed everything. At the end of the scene, if it had pleased him, he would say, 'Marvellous! Wonderful! Onwards!'

It was not only my mother whom he praised – he would praise anyone whom he thought was good. This is very important to actors. He would also make sure that actors who were giving unusually good performances, albeit a 'cough and a spit', had their fair share of the camera.

The people who had chosen the locations and designed the sets impressed her with their achievements. 'I would come along in the morning, having learned the scene, but having no idea what the set would be like. Every single set we had amazed me, because it was so different each time and so real. When I did the scene where Edna is in the mental hospital, we went to Banstead and were told that we were in Ward K. When I reached Ward K, I thought that all the patients from that ward were up and dressed and out for the day. I began to get all sentimental and said to the crew, "Oh – look at their things. Treasured photographs, little mementoes of where they used to live; each bed is different." A crew member said to me, "What are you going on about? This is a set – it has all been done by the designer." I was completely taken in, I thought it was the real thing.

'However there were genuine inmates about, a lot of them – very few are kept locked up nowadays. Anyone who can safely be let out is allowed to wander around, even go shopping. They're very often on a drug that controls them. They did show us into one ward where the patients were mentally deranged and I remember the system. We had to knock, then the door was unlocked and we were allowed in and the door was locked again behind us. The staff did not want these patients to go outside. There were various people in there. The Sister said, "Come and meet Miss Hayes, who is going to be in a film." Some of them were interested – others weren't the slightest bit interested. One woman came up, stared into my face, and then pushed me to one side. Her face was extremely battered and I asked the Sister what had happened to her,

An all-star cast in Malta for Anthony Newley's film *Can Hieronymus Merkin Ever Forget Mercy Humpe and Find True Happiness?* 1969.

The happy family — Gemma, Richard, Patricia (holding Mignon) and Teresa.

With Warren Mitchell and the fabulous Dandy Nichols in an episode of
'Till Death Us Do Part'.

thinking that she might have had a fall. The Sister said, "No – I'm afraid that was done to her by the other inmates. You see she is very, very naughty. If she can, she gets into the dining-room quickly and helps herself to all their sugar, she steals their things and always grabs the best of everything. After a time they've had enough of it and they give her a bashing." '

The venues were always interesting, a real opportunity for some insight into the lives of these unwanted people. In Blackfriars Road they worked in a building which had been until very recently a dormitory for 'down-and-out' women since Dickensian times and had hardly changed at all.

'You walked past a little kiosk where they booked you in for the night. It cost 6d (2½p). Down the corridor there was a great big old kitchen range which was alight. Here the down-and-outs could cook themselves a meal and were looked over by some helpers. Upstairs in the dormitory the beds were only about eighteen inches wide, with paper-thin, uncomfortable mattresses and just one blanket. Bitterly cold in the winter. There were little dingy windows at one end; along the sides were rows and rows of beds about two feet apart and at the other end a cupboard filled from top to bottom with enamel chamberpots.

'The building was of enormous historical interest, but it had just been sold. The new owners were in quite a quandary because they were embarrassed by the condition of it and at the same time aware that it should be preserved for posterity.'

One day the company went to Dorking to film some exterior shots but it started raining heavily. Immediately the location researchers were sent out, and came back having discovered a big empty barn that they could use to film another scene. Ted said to my mother, 'Now we are going to do that scene in the barn – the one where you sing the song.'

'OK, but I haven't learned that scene yet.'

'There's nothing to it.' Whereupon he proceeded to go right through the scene with her, line by line, explaining what was happening and the reasons why she said everything. 'Do you know the words of the song?'

'I know the words, but I'm going to make up the tune.'

'Let me hear it,' he said. So she made up an old-fashioned tune that might be sung by someone going along the road.

'Is that it?'

'Yes – or I could sing –'

'No, no, no. We'll have the first one!' He did not want to be held up with a whole lot of meaningless tunes.

They prepared the set, including lighting a bonfire, and the scene went very well. Patricia had no problem remembering the lines, as Ted had explained them so clearly. That particular scene contained one of her favourite lines: 'I like to sleep rough, that's what keeps me in good health.' They came to the song and she sang it. Afterwards somebody wrote to her saying how much they had enjoyed the song and asking for its title!

The only studio set used was for the scenes inside Holloway Jail. Security forbade any actual filming inside the prison.

Irene Shubic was the producer, responsible for the entire project, and her budget only allowed Ted Kotchev a month to complete the film. One day, after the first three and a half weeks, when they were still battling on but had not nearly finished, Irene Shubic came down to the shoot and was seen having a long serious conversation with Ted Kotchev over lunch. Afterwards he said to my mother, 'Well – the powers that be have sent a message today to say that I must be finished by the end of the week. I have said, "Right – I will finish by the end of the week, and you will have got yourselves half a movie. I can't be controlled by time. However long it takes, that is what I must take. If you want half a movie – well, we'll finish it there." '

Fortunately, he was allowed to carry on and it took six weeks. However, when he was going to direct another Jeremy Sandford play about gypsies, the producers were so rigid about the time schedule that he ultimately abandoned the whole project and returned to the other side of the Atlantic, where he is given the necessary leeway. 'I can't work like that,' he said. 'I might finish in far less time than you give me or I might take a bit longer. I cannot be pinned down to a time, because these things go along at their own pace. You get a day when you have to scrap everything you've taken, because the wrong actor has been cast in the role. You get a day when the weather and the light are totally unsuitable for the scene, and you all have to go off somewhere else. You have to do it properly, or you get badly made, cheap films.'

The scenes in the institution 'Jesus Saves' were filmed at a house in Hackney. Some of the women from the The Shelter, where Ted had taken my mother on their first meeting, were involved in the filming. They did not act or say anything, they were just sitting around in the background because they were the 'real thing'. They were background extras, and there were other extras as well. Any real parts had to be played by actors because of Equity rules. They were an interesting bunch of people in many ways, because they were all damaged. Amongst them there was a woman who seemed to be a kind of chaperone, and one day my mother asked her, 'You don't live in that hostel, do you?'

'Yes, I do. I got into the hostel because I wandered into the police station one day and said, "I've got no money and nowhere to live – can you help me?" They rang the hostel, then said, "All we can do is to send you to a hostel where there are some drunks, and some women on drugs, but they will take you in." '

My mother asked her how she came to be in such a situation and this was her story: 'Well, I lived down in Brighton with my husband and my son. My husband died very suddenly, and three weeks later my son was killed on his motor bike. They were all I had – all at once I had nothing to live for. I just took what money I had, and a small case with clothes and things that I could carry. I locked up my house and started walking. I walked – sleeping where I could – sometimes having a bed for the night – sometimes sleeping rough – right up to the North, to the Lake District. Then I started to walk back. By the time I reached London all my money had gone, and that was when I went to the police and they put me in the hostel. The women who run the place have discovered that the girls in there all relate to me; they all come and talk to me – they'll come and have a cry on my shoulder. They've offered me a job somewhere else as a hostess in one of the hostels. I now feel that I have got worth-while work to do.'

There was another girl who was only there because she was expecting a baby and had nowhere else to go. The others were fascinated by the thought of the baby growing inside her, and wanted to put their hands on her stomach when the baby was kicking.

'There was one great big girl who came up to me one day and asked if she could sit on my lap. I said, "It's no good sitting on my lap because I'm just about to start work on another scene," so she turned to actress Kate Williams and said, "Can I sit on your lap?" Kate Williams said, "All right – come on then," and this great big girl sat on Kate Williams' lap, put her arm around her neck and sucked her thumb. Just like a four-year-old, leaning on her and sucking her thumb like a baby. We knew then that that was one of the problems. Like poor Edna, they had not had the sort of love and security that a child is entitled to. Kate Williams went on to star in "Love Thy Neighbour"; she is an excellent actress and was wonderful in her part. I admired her – I did not fancy having that huge girl on my knee, but I suppose Kate was bigger than me and had a more ample lap!'

The woman who supervised 'Jesus Saves' was superbly played by Barbara Jefford. How devastating it was in the story when all her efforts were destroyed by local prejudice and the hostel had to be closed. (Hence the original title, which was to have been *Not In Our Street*.)

However, *Edna* was far from a personal tragedy for my mother. It was the beginning of a whole new phase in her career. The accolades even started when they were actually filming. During the convent scene, which was filmed at

Wonersh seminary, both teaching and trainee priests watched the shooting of the piece when Edna, under psychiatric treatment, cries pathetically for her mother, 'Mummy – Mummy!' At the end of the section, when Ted Kotchev finally shouted, 'Cut!', the priests burst into spontaneous applause. Understandably, it used to annoy Ted if a crowd gathered during the shooting and applauded before the end; he would ask them to wait until he had shouted, 'Cut.' One notable occasion when this occurred was when Edna hurled the bottle through the window of 'Jesus Saves', to the cheers of the gathered passers-by.

'However', she says, modestly, '*Edna* was bouquets all the time. I often feel when people talk about it that it wasn't only me. The part suited me and I'm not an inconsiderable actress – but I was so fortunate in having that marvellously written part with that wonderful director. I really believe that any good actress who had got the part of Edna would have made the part her own and appeared to be absolutely fantastic in it. With Ted Kotchev directing, the part was likely to win an award. Even Kathleen Harrison said to me, "You'll get an award – I haven't been in the business all these years not to recognize an award-winning part when I see one!" '

The filming was completed on my mother's birthday, 22 December 1970, but the programme did not appear until the autumn of 1971 and the Society for Film and Television Arts awards were presented in February 1972. Fortunately, my mother was very busy meanwhile.

11

The Award, Back to Stratford & the West End

During 1971 my mother was involved in two new television comedy shows: 'The Trouble With You, Lillian', co-starring Dandy Nichols, and 'The Last of the Baskets' starring Arthur Lowe and Ken Jones.

'The Trouble With You, Lillian' had originally been broadcast on the radio with Beryl Reid and my mother, and they and the director, Lesley Megahey, were very enthusiastic about it. It brought to the fore a clever young writer, Jennifer Philips. It was a marvellous study of the relationship between two women: the landlady, Madge played by Beryl Reid, and her lodger, Lillian played by my mother. They both needed the other; the lodger needed a roof over her head and the landlady needed company and somebody on whom she could take out all her grievances. There was nothing too sinister in the relationship, and it was frequently extremely funny. Although Lillian seemed to be helpless in the power of Madge, in a curious way, Lillian always got her own back; somehow things would work out her way. My mother based her character on a woman called Mrs Stillwell, whom we referred to as Nan Nan; she had helped look after us when we were children, and later she helped with my two children. The most beautiful, patient, long-suffering person, always putting duty first, she died early in 1988, and is sadly mourned by all of us.

The television version of 'The Trouble With You, Lillian' was not as successful as it should have been for a variety of reasons, which were somehow unavoidable, but my mother feels that there is still a lot of potential there and has even encouraged Jennifer Philips to take the best out of the scripts and make them into a stage play. A female version of 'The Odd Couple', perhaps.

Later in the year my mother was sent for, rather hurriedly, to take over from another actress in 'The Last of the Baskets', starring the late Arthur Lowe. They rehearsed in London, but as it was a Granada production they filmed it in Manchester. She remembers asking Arthur, 'Do you think we'll get another series at the end of this?'

'I hope not.'

'Don't you like it?'

'I don't like working in Manchester.'

'I love going to Manchester.'

'I lived there for forty years, I've only just recently got away from it. I don't want to keep going back there.'

'I like the people up there. A friend and I went into a shop the other day to return something that she had only just bought which was faulty. The assistant was absolutely charming and insisted on changing it immediately, without any cross-examination. In London you would have to prove that you had not broken the object yourself.'

Arthur agreed with that, but he still said, 'My mother lives up there and I go up to see her, but basically I look upon myself now as a Londoner. I made it to London at last!'

Once again the series was not as successful as it should have been, but my mother thoroughly enjoyed working with Arthur Lowe whom she looked upon as an extremely good actor. Ken Jones – another excellent actor, and not quite as testy as Arthur – played her son.

The year 1971 may have not have started as successfully as she would have liked, but in October *Edna* was televised and received with tremendous acclaim. One critic said: 'Miss Hayes will now have to be looked on in a different light and considered for more dramatic roles.'

'I realized that, when *Edna* came out, there was a good chance that I would be looked on as a serious actress. I suppose one of the reasons that I had not been so successful before was that in many ways I did not want to be. I never went into the theatre with the idea of being a big success; I went into it with the idea of being able to do a variety of different parts. I did not want to be stuck doing the same thing all the time. Outside of that there is only the money. Where else could I have commanded such good money for such personal pleasure? My next-door-neighbour, Celia French, asked me when I was going to retire and I had to reply that I would be crazy to retire at all, unless I was not well enough to carry on. I said to Warren Mitchell, one day, "I'm thinking of buying a little house in Australia, near my daughter Teresa, for my retirement." He said, "You'll never retire – you'll drop dead on the boards." Of course, that's every actor's dream.'

People suddenly realized that she was not just a stooge to the comedians, but a fine actress in her own right. They can be forgiven for having had the wrong impression, because it had been many years since she had devoted herself to serious acting – and most of her audience would have been too young to remember her as anything but a comedy actress who worked with the comics.

'I am not a comedienne. I am an actress who has learned to play comedy. So is Warren Mitchell, he is a great actor who plays comedy very well, especially the harsh, biting material that Johnny Speight writes. John Cleese is an actor, so was Tony Hancock. John le Mesurier was another, Deryck Guyler and Frank Thornton. The numbers are endless.'

Edna went out in October 1971, and the following February we were all sitting on the edge of our seats at the Albert Hall, awaiting the announcement and presentation of the Society for Film and Television Arts Awards (now the British Academy of Film and Television Arts [BAFTA] Awards).

When the four nominations for 'Best Actress of the Year' were read out, my mother's name was among them and the next few minutes seemed like an eternity. 'The Award for Best Actress of the Year goes to Patricia Hayes for her outstanding performance in *Edna the Inebriate Woman*.' A roar of applause went up from the theatrical audience; she looked so proud and strangely unemotional and we were all in tears.

Later in the year, when she won 'Best Actress' in the the *Sun* newspaper awards, I was overwhelmed to hear Edward Woodward, who was also picking up an award, say 'Some actors don't like awards, but when you see someone like Patricia Hayes, whom we have all known as a really good actress for years, when you see her at last receive an award, you know that they are worth having.' He did not even mention his own.

Immediately after the presentations the flowers, letters and phone calls began flooding in. There were telegrams from many people she had worked with during her career, such as Peter Sellers and Spike Milligan. She was bombarded with congratulations and appreciation from colleagues, friends and admirers from every walk of life. The most overwhelming emotion was that they were thrilled to see someone who had given her whole life to the theatre finally reap the benefits and prove herself worthy of such a wonderful opportunity.

Margaret Lockwood was another of Herbert de Leon's clients. Herbert rang my mother one day: 'Patricia, dear, Margaret Lockwood is going on tour in a Noël Coward play, *Relative Values*. There is a very nice part in it for you. Angela Baddeley played it originally. I think it would suit you. Also it will consolidate the fact that you are a straight actress.'

Gemma had just left drama school and my mother arranged for her to have an audition for the little maid's part in *Relative Values*. She got the part, and it enabled her to obtain her coveted Equity membership. However she also had to do some stage management as well, which made her a

little indignant since she had studied with people who speci-
fically wanted to be stage managers, and she felt she was doing
them out of a job. This was obviously an economy on the part
of the management. Gemma did not complete the tour
because, half-way through, she contracted mumps, and she
was too ill to continue.

While the rehearsals for *Relative Values* were in progress, an
old schoolfriend of mine, actress Pauline Collins, was selected
to be a victim on 'This Is Your Life' and my mother and I were
both asked to be involved in the programme. I shall always
remember Pauline turning to Eamonn Andrews when he said,
'Pauline Collins, This Is Your Life,' and saying, 'But I have no
life!' She felt that she was too young to be a subject. However,
while they were preparing Pauline's life, one of the organizers
said, 'This is ridiculous! Here we are with Patricia Hayes
appearing on Pauline's Life, and we have never done her Life.'
Immediately plans were swung into action, all in the utmost
secrecy.

Having contacted as many stars, old colleagues, friends and
relatives as possible, they decided on a plan of campaign to
catch her unawares. The rehearsals for *Relative Values* were
being held at the Globe Theatre during the day and there was
also a play being performed there at night. The cast of
Relative Values were warned that, on a particular evening,
the BBC would be televising an excerpt from the other play,
in an attempt to improve its ticket sales. They were told to
take no notice of the crew who would be setting up cameras
and lighting. Funnily enough, my mother did think that it
was a little strange, as she had seen an excerpt from that very
play not all that long ago; however, she was not in the least
suspicious. Then the cast were told to bring in something special to wear after rehearsals that same day,
since a photographer was coming in to take some publicity
shots.

On the designated day, at 5 p.m., the producer Clive Swift
said, 'You can all go home now, except Patricia and Margaret.
I want to rehearse their scene.'

My mother piped up quickly 'But what about our photo call?'

'Oh, yes, everyone – don't forget the photo call!' he said quickly, hoping that his mistake had given nothing away. Joyce Blair, who was also in the play, quickly combed my mother's hair and put a little make-up on her, 'To make her pretty for the photos!'

'Start the scene,' said Clive Swift, 'and don't stop; I want to get a good run on it with the two of you. By the way, if the lights come up, take no notice, it's those blessed people preparing for tonight's televisation. Just carry on.'

'We started acting hammer and tongs,' recalls Patricia. 'The lights came up as expected, then I became aware that somebody was edging up beside me on my left, but I carried on until a voice suddenly said, "I'm sorry to interrupt you" and I looked around and there stood Eamonn Andrews with the big red book in his hands and I said, "Oh Margaret, it's going to be your Life," but he said, "No – Patricia Hayes – Award-Winning Actress. This Is Your Life." I laughed and laughed to think how I had been tricked into it.

'When they did my Life, I had a very enjoyable evening with a succession of comedians, but afterwards I thought, "That wasn't really my life. They left people like Nan Nan out, she should have come on with my two grandchildren, Katie and Thomas." '

Relative Values opened at the Lyceum Theatre in Edinburgh and toured for ten weeks. My mother enjoyed the part; the standard of acting was very high and it was a pleasure working with such a professional actress as Margaret Lockwood, but in general it was a lonely and rather unhappy time for her. She had no particular friend, and Gemma, quite naturally, was busy with the young people in the company. She had originally thought that it would give her an opportunity to escape from all the attention she had been receiving since *Edna*. She had had to come to terms with people shouting, 'Hey – Edna!' everywhere she went, coming up to her in the street nudging her, wanting autographs the minute she stood still for a moment anywhere. Presumably, because you appear in their lounge, television audiences feel that they own their celebrities and know them personally. My mother fondly imagined that she would not be so well known outside London. She was in for a massive shock. The London public were tame compared to the people in the provinces, who were even more thrilled to see a real live celebrity and rushed at her in the street.

'Nobody in the cast wanted to be with me, I held them up all the time. Also it's awfully annoying to be constantly walking around with someone who is being fêted all the time when you may be playing a better part in the play. Receiving public acclaim is a side of the business I was quite unused to, and it is still an aspect that I have problems coming to terms with. As Fate would have it, I also became unwell.

'One day, when I was in the middle of a scene with Margaret and one or two others in the play, I suddenly felt as if all sound was gradually receding away from me, getting fainter and fainter. It felt as if I was shut off from everybody, in a vacuum and the whole world – not visually but soundwise – seemed to be vanishing further and further away. I thought "In a minute, I'm not going to be able to go on and the other members of the cast will ask me what is wrong." I hung on and hung on until suddenly the curtain came down and it was the end of the act. Even then, the cast left the set in the normal way laughing and chatting to each other, leaving me bewildered and alone. They hadn't realized that anything was wrong. The stage crew had to ask me to move, in order for them to do their scene change, because I was still standing there as if I was stunned. When I was safely back in my dressing-room, I said to Gemma, who happened to come in, "I think I had a very slight stroke out there." "Why?" "I just felt as if I was going – not faint or sick – as if my brain was becoming detached from reality." Unbeknown to me, Gemma contacted the management and in between the two shows (it was a matinée) a lovely old Liverpool doctor came to visit me. After examining me he said, "You can put your mind to rest about a stroke. I may be sticking my neck out, but you are the most unlikely person to have a stroke because your blood pressure is absolutely normal, extra-ordinarily normal for someone of your age. I think that you have a touch of Ménière's Disease. Don't worry about it, because we can control it. It shouldn't stop you working at all." '

Fortunately, the tablets he prescribed were completely successful and she was able to control it. Others who have the same disorder call the attacks their 'mazy fits' because it feels as if they are in a maze. Fortunately, too, my mother no longer has the attacks; maybe the stress induced them.

A diary entry on 31 January 1973 reads 'Ron Eyre'. During the tour of *Relative Values* she was offered a part by the impres-ario Michael Codran in a new play by Alan Bennett, *Habeas Corpus*, about to be put on in the West End.

'I was sent the script to read. When I read it, I found it was so scripted that it was awfully difficult to know how anybody could possibly direct it. There were no formal entrances or exits. After I had read it, I rang Herbert de Leon saying that I did not want to do it. He said, "Patricia, dear, this is a West End, Michael Codran production – you will be crazy if you don't accept it!" So I agreed to do it. "There's an appointment booked for you to meet the director, Ron Eyre, at the end of this week as soon as you have finished the tour." '

Ron Eyre's first words to her were, 'This is exciting, isn't it?'

'Yes,' she said, half wondering if 'exciting' was quite the word she would have chosen. 'How are you going to stage it, because there are no entrances or exits in the script?' she asked anxiously.

'You know, that's the sixty-four thousand dollar question. How do *you* envisage the part of Mrs Swab?'

'What do you want?'

'I'm not sure – but what we don't want is the little woman you are always playing.'

That was a blow because now she did not know what he was

after. 'I'm a very good reader, Ron, but it sometimes takes me a while to become as good as I want to be in a part, on stage. My first reading and my hundredth performance come together.'

'Now she tells me!'

The rehearsal period was only a month. The National Theatre does not expect actors to be ready in four weeks, but will allow six to eight weeks for a play that seems relatively simple. In the past, even in the commercial theatre, plays that were coming in to the West End would always go on a long tour, by the end of which everyone had fully come to grips with their characters. Nowadays, because everything is so much more expensive, including the actors (who have to be paid a full wage from the first day of rehearsals) managements simply cannot afford longer rehearsal time or support the enormous cost of a long tour. 'I sometimes think that employees very often institute bargains which suit them, but which lead to massive unemployment among their colleagues and in the end they kill the goose that laid the golden egg.'

There was a fabulous cast for *Habeas Corpus*, headed by Sir Alec Guinness, with Joan Sanderson, Phyllida Law, Margaret Courtenay, Eric Thompson, Andrew Sachs, John Bird, Madeleine Smith and Roddy Maud-Roxby. The play was an enormous hit and my visit to it one of the funniest evenings I have ever spent. However, it was not all plain sailing at the beginning. Firstly my poor mother caught a virulent flu germ and was feeling terribly ill during the final rehearsals at Oxford where the play was tried out. There was even some doubt about whether she would be on for the first night.

'The rehearsals were traumatic. It was an extremely difficult part, the dialogue was impossible to learn, and there was no place where I could say, "I leave the stage here, because I am going out to the kitchen." Ron did not want anything established. There were three bays on each side of the stage and he would say, "Exit left-hand, bay two, or right-hand, bay one." You went off through one exit and came on from another. For the first fifty performances there was a stage manager each side of the stage whose job it was, as I came off, to tell me which bay to go to. It's to their credit that they always sent me to the right one. I'll tell you how difficult it was, and this is proof of it:

'When Sir Alec decided to come out of the play after the first nine months, I came out as well. Sir Alec said to me one night, "Do you know who is going to take over your part?" and I said "No." "Have a guess." I guessed at one or two obvious people and then gave up. He said, "The Author!" "You mean Alan Bennett himself?" "Yes." "That's funny, because someone once told me that he wrote the part of Mrs Swab for himself." "He wrote all the parts for himself," said Sir Alec, wittily.

'So Alan Bennett took over my part, and he was probably very good in it – although I never saw him. One night, while we were still finishing the run and the new cast were rehearsing, Sir Alec threw a champagne party in his dressing-room for the old cast to meet the new cast. In came Alan Bennett. I had always felt, all through the rehearsals, that he was not very happy with what I was doing with Mrs Swab and that he avoided me. However, on this occasion when he saw me he made a bee-line for me, enveloped me in his arms and said passionately, "I had no idea when I wrote it, how horrendously difficult the part of Mrs Swab was. I hadn't a clue. What you must have gone through! I know because I am going through it now. I don't know which side I go on or which side I go off. I don't know how to say the lines – it is horrendous." '

How grateful she was when he said that! After she came out of the play she received a letter from Michael Codran, which read, 'Thank you so much for the good work. I don't think any of us realized at the time what an extremely difficult part Mrs Swab would turn out to be!'

'It was the most difficult part I had ever had to do to. I felt that Ron Eyre was completely and utterly disappointed in me. One day during rehearsals I said to him, "How do you see the part – what manner do you see it being played in?"

He looked puzzled for a moment, and then said, "Well –
Shakespearian." I thought, *Shakespearian*? I was a housekeeper who discussed things like hoovering the floor and the
menu she had served for dinner that night. It wasn't until I'd
been playing it for quite some time that I realized what he
meant. In fact, the whole play needs to be given the
Shakespearian treatment – even the little salesman who is
selling false boobs to the flat-chested sister needs a sort of
Shakespearian style. The play was almost entirely made up of
well-known phrases or sayings. All intricately woven together
to make a play. A brilliant piece of writing – hilariously funny.
Ron Eyre's production was quite unique and, although it must
have been a nightmare for him in the early stages, the results
were astoundingly good. There were some magnificent performances from the cast: Sir Alec was, as ever, a tower of
strength, Joan Sanderson always a jewel, playing the permanently aggravating woman that she does so well. She had
one of the most memorable lines in the play. When asked if she
knew who was the father of her illegitimate child, conceived
during an air raid, she admits that it was difficult to see who it
was, 'through the haze of a post-coital Craven A'. It was the
first time many of us became aware of Andrew Sachs, who was
to create the character of the Spanish waiter, Manuel,
in the comedy series 'Fawlty Towers.' Margaret Courtenay
was quite exceptionally good as Sir Alec's overpowering
wife.'

Despite the problems with the play itself, the cast was a
happy one and my mother learned a great deal and grew
enormously within the part. She would not give up perfecting
the role. There was one short scene with John Bird that she
absolutely dreaded. One night she came off and said to him,
'We got it right tonight – this scene has always worried me,'
and he said, 'It has always worried me, too.' That night they
had suddenly discovered how to play it, and from then
onwards it always worked for them.

ITV's 1975 entry for the Montreux Festival was a half-hour

comedy play, commissioned from Ray Galton and Alan Simpson.

'The play was called *Holiday With Strings* and starred Les Dawson. Patricia recalls: 'It was a story about a guy who goes on a shoddy package holiday to Spain. Strangely enough, one of the jokes was that someone had to do a whip-round on the plane to buy petrol for the flight – and a couple of weeks ago it really happened! A case of real life copying art. We used an old Bristol freighter, which looked ancient, but which was of course a perfectly good plane. We had patches on the tyres just as they do in *Comic Cuts*. The passengers had to climb up a ladder to get into the plane, and everything was very tatty.' Pat played the air hostess, and she was wonderful. She pushed a trolley up and down the plane selling raffle tickets; the prize for the winners was lunch, which consisted of fish and chips, literally thrown at them by Pat! It was a very funny little film, and won third prize at Montreux. Pat is a godsend to any writer. We used to laugh just to see her, so little and elfin and with such a mischievous quality about her. At rehearsals she is always so charming, with a delightful laugh. Of course writers of comedy love actors who can't stop laughing at their scripts and with Pat it was always totally genuine. She is a very generous artist – never any question of trying to upstage her fellow actors.'

Ray Galton and Johnnie Speight also wrote the first episode of an intended series called 'The Tea-ladies'. It starred my mother and Dandy Nichols as two outrageous tea-ladies who worked at the House of Commons. What a brilliant idea! These two women were serving tea to all the extremely important politicians without the slightest respect for any of them, scope for tremendous political satire. Squabbling over who should make the Prime Minister's tea, and passing rude personal comments about all the famous MPs of the day.

Unfortunately, the BBC wanted to make cuts and alterations to the scripts, and Galton and Speight complained to journalists that the BBC was censoring them and trying to intimidate them. It became a very bitter quarrel, conducted in the pages of the national press. After this public slanging-match, Galton and Speight did not write any more scripts – which meant that the first episode was the first and last of what could have become an extremely amusing and popular series.

Out of the blue, my mother was suddenly sent for, to go and see Peter Gill about a part in the next season at Stratford. He wanted her to appear in his production of *Twelfth Night* which was to open in Stratford before coming to London for a season at the Aldwych. (This was before the Royal Shakespeare Company had their new home in the Barbican Complex.)

When Peter Gill asked her to play Maria she was startled. 'Surely, I am too old.'

'No, you are not, if you read the play properly. Anybody who understands the play as I do will realize that Maria is, in fact, an older woman. She's a gentlewoman, and she's obviously been with the family, of which Olivia is now the only remaining member, for many years. Olivia's father having died, and her brother being presumed lost at sea, she has engaged a new steward, Malvolio. It has to be made plain that Malvolio is new to the household, and the reason that Maria plays such a cruel trick on him is because he is so pompous and gives himself such airs, but above all, because he berates her in front of Sir Toby Belch, with whom she has obviously been in love for years and years and years.'

'But she's nearly always played by a buxom young girl.'

'Yes – and I'll tell you why. Viola is dressed as a boy, and Olivia is cold and distant, until she mistakenly falls madly in love with Viola. Modern people have come to look for a little sex in a play, so producers thought it would be a good idea to make Maria into a sexy, buxom wench with big boobs, playing a mischievous character. It is completely wrong for the play. The whole play has an undertone of sadness. Everyone is longing for someone else, someone unobtainable. Maria is one of the few who eventually get what they're longing for. Sir Toby marries her after she has got him out of a scrape.'

'I'd love to come to Stratford and play Maria, if you think I'm right for it. I have not been to Stratford for forty years.'

'Well, go and see Trevor Nunn in his office; he is expecting you.'

Trevor Nunn was delighted, and said that they would be very happy to have her. He also offered her the part of one of the witches, in his production of *Macbeth*. She was thrilled, but warned, 'The only trouble is that I have got two dogs.'

'That's no problem, we'll find somewhere for you to stay where they'll be happy for you to have the dogs with you. Beatrix Lehmann brought three cats when she came down last year, and she had a very happy time.'

Trevor Nunn conceived a most interesting production of *Macbeth*. The other Witches were played by Jane Lapotaire and Anne Dyson. Each of them decided how she was going to play her witch. Jane Lapotaire said 'My witch is going to be young, pregnant, semi-blind and imbecilic. Sensing things out of the atmosphere.'

'My witch is going to be old, and a really wicked, scheming hag,' said my mother. Last, but by no means least, Anne Dyson said, 'Mine is going to be even older than Patricia's, and on the verge of losing her powers.'

The curtain was to go up and reveal the three witches in a magic circle. It was not until half-way through the rehearsal period that Trevor Nunn announced to the three witches that a stainless steel ring, about four feet in diameter, was going to be lowered on wires from the darkness of the flies. They then had to sit on it as best they could, hanging on to each other and any available wires, while they were whisked up, so that they loomed above the heads of all the other actors. From that magic circle he wanted them to conjure up a huge thunderstorm.

'I don't know how to conjure up a storm,' my mother told him.

'I shall not tell you how to conjure up a storm. I leave it to the three of you.'

What a storm they conjured! The air was rent with the sounds of jarring, stammering, moaning and cackling and screaming that built to a huge crescendo, only relieved by the most enormous crack of thunder. As time went on their noises became more mysterious and strident and witchlike and terrifying. Later, when they came to London, several of the parts were re-cast so Trevor had to re-rehearse the play.

'Let's do another run-through,' said Trevor; they had already done three.

'Can we leave out conjuring up the storm? We've done it so many times at Stratford, and here we'll save time if we just leave it out and come to the end of it and start with the thundersheets.'

Trevor looked at her aghast. 'Patricia – I can't believe it. I've watched you over the last weeks and months conjuring up the most amazing thunderstorms, and now you say to me that you are sick of it and can you leave it out? No, you certainly cannot leave it out! I insist on another thunderstorm.'

My mother absolutely loved living and working in Stratford. Everybody came to see the plays, and she was found perfect accommodation where her two dogs were welcome. 'I had a tiny little house, with a sitting room and kitchen downstairs, and a bedroom and bathroom upstairs. It adjoined another little house and they were both in the grounds of a converted farmhouse owned by Ian and Dee Currall. Ian and Dee were so good to me that we have remained friends ever since. They had two small children at the time, the eldest was called David and was 4 years old. David would come into my house and say, "I'll hoover your stairs for you," or he would come in when I was learning my lines and say, "When shall we free meet again?" One day I said to his mother, "Would David like to come to a matinée of the show? I don't know whether he'll be able to stay for the whole play, he'd get bored, but I'll ask the management if he can just come in, if somebody sits with him, to watch the witches' scene." It was all arranged and he was so longing to see it. A charming house manager offered to take him into a box and sit with him where he could see me very clearly. The curtain went up, and down we came on the magic circle, I glanced towards the box and there was this little pale face, with huge blue eyes gazing at me as we ranted, "When shall we three meet again?" By the next scene he had gone.

'Dee was wonderful to me. Sometimes I would come back after rehearsing all day, and with a show to perform at night. She would put her head out of her door, which was opposite mine, and ask, "Got a show tonight?" "Yes." "Have you eaten?" "No." "Come in, I've got food ready." '

The casts for both the plays were full of extremely talented actors: Nicol Williamson, so arrogant and conceited as Malvolio that we could afford to laugh heartily at his demise; Helen Mirren, exciting and utterly spontaneous as Lady Macbeth; Ron Pember, the perfect comic/tragic figure as Feste, with a lovely tuneful singing voice for his soulful songs; Richard Griffiths, who was there for his first season, an amazingly gifted actor capable of playing any age from twenty-five upwards; Frank Thornton, whose ability took many people by surprise because they tended to think of him, like my mother, solely in terms of television comedy: Jane Lapotaire, an extremely versatile actress who later went on to play Edith Piaf in the musical *Piaf*; the late Gordon Jackson. It was the first time my mother had worked with this charming and delightful man, who later worked with my son (her grandson, obviously) Tom Jennings, who is now an established actor in Australia.

People sometimes ask my mother what she likes playing best, and she admits that Shakespeare is her first love. At drama school she was considered to be exceptionally good at it, and it holds no fears for her. Many people feel that, because it is in verse and not in prose, it is going to be awkward and difficult to speak. A few minutes with my mother on the subject will soon allay any fears. When I asked her what role she would like to play she said, 'I would love to play Titania. I think that fairies are as old as the world. A little old Titania and a little old Oberon would have a genuinely ethereal and unhuman quality. But whatever the part, I would give anything to go back to Stratford for another season if I were free – and of course if they asked me.'

12

'Till Death Us Do Part' &
Katharine Hepburn

Early in 1975, another hilarious series of 'Till Death Us Do Part' was screened. Johnny Speight's scripts were brilliant and once again Warren Mitchell was superb as the opinionated and discontented Alf Garnett. The author John Osborne once described Alf Garnett as Johnny Speight's Falstaff. My mother was engaged to play his irritating next-door neighbour, Min, with Alfie Bass as her extremely hen-pecked husband. Min was portrayed as a nympho-maniac, always trying to arouse her husband's non-existent sex drive by putting aphrodisiacs in his food. But to no avail. Bert was not the slightest bit interested in that side of life with anyone, least of all with her! In one episode Min and Bert went round to watch the Muhammad Ali fight with the Garnetts. Min took with her a goldfish bowl in which she was convinced that the spirit of her Uncle Fred, who was dead, had returned as a goldfish. She could tell by looking at him. She knew that Uncle Fred would have given anything to watch the fight, so she sat there, much to the annoyance of Alf Garnett, holding the goldfish bowl all through the fight.

When the show was over one of the props men asked my mother 'Do you want those two goldfish?'

'No thank you, I haven't got anywhere to put them. I

don't have a pond.'

'Oh, all right – never mind.'

'What do you mean, never mind? What will happen to them?'

'Oh, well – we'll just sling them down the drain.'

'You can't do that – I'll have them.' So she took them home.

'When I got home I wondered what to do with them, and then I remembered that the three men who lived next door had a goldfish pond in their garden. I went straight to their house and said, "I've brought two goldfish round who have just starred in the Alf Garnett show. This big one here, with all the fringes and things is called Uncle Fred; the other one has not got a name. Will you have them?" They were quite happy to have them, and we put them in the necessary polythene bag, which gradually takes on the exact temperature of the pond water, before they were finally released. (A sudden change of temperature can be fatal to goldfish.) Every now and then, I would enquire about the two goldfish, and the reply would be, "We don't know about the other one, because he looks the same as ours, but Uncle Fred is still going strong. He sometimes pops up to the surface and looks at us." '

The men-next-door moved recently, and we understand that Uncle Fred is enjoying his new life in Brighton!

The basic team of 'Till Death' consisted of Warren Mitchell, Dandy Nichols, Una Stubbs and Anthony Booth. The director was Dennis Main Wilson. Rehearsals were frequently livened up by the most terrible rows between Warren Mitchell and Dennis Main Wilson – the reason for these we will come to shortly.

Dennis Main Wilson was one of the bright boys of post-war radio, responsible among other programmes for 'The Goon Show' and 'Hancock's Half Hour'. He later made the inevitable change to BBC Television with successes such as 'Marty', 'The Rag Trade' and 'Till Death Us Do Part'. He is known for his dynamic energy, almost to the point of lunacy, for his ability to make sweeping changes where necessary and – last, but by no means least – for the fact that ninety per cent of his calorie intake would be alcohol. He has an amazing capacity to hold his drink; only those who know him very well would be able to say with any accuracy, 'You're pissed mate.'

'I remember once,' recalls my mother, 'when Dennis and Warren had the most appalling row, shouting at each other. Una Stubbs turned to me: "This is what Dandy could not bear," and I said, "Yes – I know – but I love it." Una whispered, "So do I." I love a big row as long as I'm not involved in it. It is wonderful to hear two people going for each other hammer and tongs and really speaking their minds.'

The reason for the rows is summed up by Warren. He was not afraid to tell Dennis, too, at the top of his voice. 'You are one person in the morning, and another person altogether after lunch. So let us please from now on rehearse in the mornings only. We'll all come in two hours earlier if you like, and rehearse straight through until 2 p.m. without lunch, because when you go to the pub (or to the "bank", as you put it) another man comes back afterwards. A totally different and utterly incompetent man! Who do you think you are kidding when you say you are going to the bank? Have they started serving whisky at the bank?'

'How dare you speak to me like that? How *dare* you?' bellowed Dennis.

'I dare because I have got to, Dennis. We cannot go on with a maniac telling us what to do in the afternoons. What you said to Pat just now was rubbish – absolute rubbish.'

'Very well! Very well! If that's how you feel I'll leave – I shall go,' stormed Dennis dramatically.

'No – I'm going!' screamed Warren, not to be outdone.

'No, you are not – *I'm* going!'

Warren is the most professional of actors and even though he was playing Alf Garnett – a man capable of the ultimate in bad manners – he would never have spoken to any director in that fashion without the most unbelievable provocation.

It was enlightening and necessary to have a long chat with Warren about these episodes before writing this section of the book. Warren says: 'Dennis Main Wilson had a marvellous track-record with the BBC, and it was by no means accidental. He had enormous enthusiasm and a tremendous ability to discover talent. For example, he discovered the inimitable Kenneth Williams while he was playing the Dauphin in *St Joan* at the Arts Theatre. I owe Dennis a great deal, he saw me playing quite an insignificant part in *The Walrus and the Carpenter* with Felix Aylmer and Hugh Griffith, when I was only a small-part player. Many people were suggested for the part of Alf Garnett when it was first written, but Dennis had seen me and he plumped for me.

'Dennis never enjoys anything if it is simple and straightforward. He offered me a part in a play once, and I accepted without hesitation because I was not working. This really frustrated Dennis; he wanted to come round and beg me to play the part. He was always very dramatic and has a clipped, military way of speaking – wanting to run the show like a complicated army manoeuvre. Take the time when he heard that Duncan Wood was thinking of using a helicopter for "Steptoe and Son" – immediately *he* had to have a helicopter. Johnny Speight, who was in the helicopter with him, said that Dennis accused the pilot of cowardice because he was reluctant to fly lower than five hundred feet. They were flying around the cranes in the dock area at the time!

'Johnny wrote one episode in which the Garnetts were playing Monopoly. Alf began to get delusions of grandeur because he owned Mayfair. It was a very funny script, but Johnny had written it in a slapdash way – having me throwing the dice and then, two lines later, throwing the dice again so I re-wrote the lines to make sense of the game. Johnny, who is now a teetotaller, used to enjoy a big night out on Saturdays, with the Fulham Football Team, at the Queen's Elm. We were rehearsing on the Sunday morning, and the run-through was seven minutes too long. Dennis Main Wilson, in his clipped voice, said: "Break. Send the car for our author." Now Johnny Speight was absolutely unapproachable on Sunday mornings. He arrived in the freezing cold Sulgrave Boys' Hall, Shepherd's Bush, wearing his camel-hair coat, smoking a Gauloise, and asked for a coffee. We started the run-through and Johnny, who never whispered, said loudly in his broad cockney accent, "I never wrote that – what's he putting lines in for? You drag me out of bed on a Sunday to cut the show! Just take the lines out." Whereupon I said, "I put the lines in, Johnny, because you didn't write the Monopoly game in properly." "It don't matter, it's dramatic licence." "I don't believe that word – dramatic licence." Suddenly up piped Dennis "Great! That's what I like! My wonderful star and my writer arguing. That's what makes the show so great – passion!" "Don't give me all that crap, Dennis", says Johnny with some forthrightness. "You drag me out of bed on a fucking Sunday morning to cut the show, and he's putting lines in. Just take the fucking lines out!" "Wonderful – wonderful – conflict!" It was life's blood to Dennis.' And in the team spirit of the show, Warren kept his new lines – and stopped the show with the scene the following night.

'Dennis, when he was sober, was quite wonderful. His camera work was often brilliant. There were those classic ad lib moments in the show when he would cut away to a shot of Dandy (the silly moo), just at the right moment and get an enormous laugh. There are not many directors of comedy who have that instinctive feel for timing.

'The most amazing thing about Dennis was his enthusiasm. For him every show was the most important show he had ever done in his life. He so loved the work, they used to take bets at the pub on how long it would take for him to get around to talking about 'Till Death'. For example, two people might be talking about parachuting, and one would say, "I think it's terribly brave to jump out of a plane with a parachute." Dennis would chip in, "Yes – brave – brave is what we need. You see we were brave when we did 'Till Death Us Do Part'." Someone would have to fork out two quid. They had lost – it had only taken him ten seconds to get on to his favourite subject.'

'Dennis is the most extraordinary man,' says my mother. 'I think he is fuelled almost entirely on whisky. I never saw him eat anything. Sometimes, after he'd had a few drinks, he would ring me up and have a long conversation with me – the content of which he would have completely forgotten the next day.'

Apparently nearly all the regulars in the programme were staunch Labour voters, and, during the rehearsal breaks, they would have tremendous political discussions and arguments. Warren Mitchell relates: 'Patricia voted Liberal, and occasionally she would gallantly take on the lot of us. On one particular afternoon the discussion became extremely heated and she finally shouted, "You lot don't know what the fuck you are talking about." We were surprised to hear her say it, and she could not believe that she had said it herself. She quickly followed it up with, "I'm so sorry – I never said 'fuck' until I joined the Royal Shakespeare Company!" How often we have quoted that wonderful line since that day!'

The series was extremely demanding, but it was also rewarding; and she thoroughly enjoyed having another opportunity to work with these truly professional actors, and with Dennis Main Wilson – in the mornings!

Bernie Stringle, a television producer with whom my mother had worked on several occasions, contacted her later that year. He had obtained the rights to Somerset Maugham's lurid first novel, *Liza of Lambeth*, and converted it into a musical, writing the lyrics himself, with music by Cliff Adams. He had already found all his financial backing and Ben Arbeid had agreed to produce it. 'I'm putting on a musical version of *Liza of Lambeth*, and I'd like you to play her mother. You will have your own song, entitled "Red Jollop".'

'I've never been in a musical before, nor sung a song. Not since I was a child and did "On Our 'Oneymoon" with my brother Brian!'

'You'll be able to do it.'

A tape of all the musical numbers, hurriedly put together with session singers, was sent to her. She was amazed at the brilliance of their rendering, and found it almost impossible to believe that they were sight-reading. In fact, a lot of singers who are proficient sight-readers make a good living in this way.

'Having read the script and heard the music I accepted the part, and progress was under way. An unlimited amount of money was spent on the scenery, the costumes and the cast. Angela Richards was to play Liza. She is a very talented actress, with a beautiful singing voice, and is also a lovely person. A darling girl called Tina Martin played her chum, and my old friend Michael Robbins her father.

The show did not prosper, though in many ways it seems it should have. The story was compelling and broken up with plenty of fun; the music was catchy and the singing and acting first-rate. My mother need not have worried about her song. After a session with the composer, Cliff Adams, she gave a rollicking rendering of 'Red Jollop'.

Hugh Leonard adapted Norman Collins' novel, *London Belongs to Me*, into a seven-part television series for Thames Television. The story is based around a lodging-house in London after the Depression between the two World Wars. The landlady is rather a tyrant and, apart from a husband and wife with two children, the lodgers are almost all eccentric, and in some cases sinister, characters. My mother was hired to play the part of Connie, a faded, peroxided would-be actress who works as a cloakroom attendant at a night-club. Connie is a tragically lonely figure, with very few friends, who is persecuted by Madge, the landlady. However, Connie's funny ways made her very amusing to watch; for example she was invited to a wedding and, when nobody was looking, proceeded to fill her handbag with food. The other actors in the series were Peter Jeffrey, Derek Farr, Madge Ryan, John Smart, Trevor Eve and Fiona Gray, not forgetting the canary. One day the canary escaped; you can imagine the problems of having a bird flying round a studio!

'Nobody could catch it, but I had owned a few canaries and knew what to do. I said, "Get a very long pole, and follow the canary everywhere with it. He will keep flying away from the long pole until eventually he will be exhausted and drop to the ground, and you will be able to pick him up." They followed my instructions, and when he fell to the ground, I was able to pick him up myself, unhurt.'

Fiona Gray, a delightful actress, extremely pretty and gifted, played a young girl in *London Belongs to Me*. Her family lived in Scotland, and Fiona was looking for accommodation. While she was searching for somewhere to rent, my mother offered to let her stay at her house for a little while. How important timing is in life! At that same point a young relative of mine by marriage, William Ramsay, offered to decorate my mother's hall, to earn some money during his university vacation. He had to spend a lot of time on the landing outside Fiona's bedroom, painting. William and Fiona are now married and have three beautiful children.

During the filming of *London Belongs to Me*, my mother was asked to go and see Franco Zeffirelli with regard to playing Joan Plowright's housekeeper in a play. The message went back that she was too busy filming, and could not manage to see him. When the series was over she took me and my two children, Katie and Tom, for a lovely surfing holiday in Cornwall. She has always adored the seaside and still plays like a child on a surfboard. On the last day of the holiday we came up off the beach to be told by the hotel receptionist that her manager had been trying to contact her all day. A script of the play was waiting for her at home, to read on the Sunday; would she please meet Franco Zeffirelli with the producer of the play, Helen Montague, on the Monday.

We arrived home on Saturday night, and on Sunday

morning she read the script of Edouardo di Filippo's
Filumena in two hours. The minute she had finished it, she
telephoned Helen Montague. 'I love the play. I think it will
be an enormous success, but I don't want to play the part.'

'You mean you don't want to work with Franco Zeffirelli!'

'I would love to work with Franco Zeffirelli, but I don't
want to keep on playing this same little old woman who lives
in the background of other people's lives. I'll be bored out of
my mind with it, Helen.'

'I think, out of courtesy, you should meet him. Be outside
the Italian Institute tomorrow morning at 11 o'clock.'

Very much against her will, she drove to Clapham Junction
the next morning and took the train to Victoria, walking
from there to the Italian Institute.

'As I approached the Institute I saw two people chatting on
the corner. One was a distinguished-looking man with
silvery hair, and the other was a woman. They watched me
crossing the road, and then Helen Montague said, "Oh, there
you are, darling!" – although we'd never met before. "Can I
introduce you to Franco Zeffirelli? Franco, this is Patricia
Hayes." I immediately felt the warmth of his tremendous
charismatic personality. "How do you do?" he said. "Now,
what do you want to do – start rehearsing immediately, or
come inside and talk?" "I want to come inside and talk," I
told him firmly. "All right, we'll go inside." '

She looked around to see where Helen Montague was, and
caught sight of her just stepping into a taxi. Perhaps she could
not face the thought of my mother turning the part down.
Franco Zeffirelli took my mother downstairs for a coffee.
'Patricia, about the part of Rosalia – *Filumena* is a play that
has been done many times in Italy, and Rosalia was always
played by a very famous Italian actress called Tina Pica.
Rosalia is *not* just a little woman in the background of other
people's lives, she is a very important character. The play is
like a three-legged stool. There are Don Domenico and
Filumena, but they cannot be the centre of interest all the
time, and there are two very important scenes for Rosalia.

Now come along, we will go up and and rehearse.'

They went straight upstairs to the room where the rehearsals were being held. There was no more discussion about whether or not my mother would play the part. She was under the magnetic spell of Franco Zeffirelli. The rest of the cast were all introduced to her – Joan Plowright, Colin Blakely, Trevor Eve (with whom she had just finished working), Larry Lamb, Christopher Guard and Larry Noble – then Franco said: 'Patricia, as you are late joining the company I will act the part for you, once. After that you must find your own way to do it.' She sat there spellbound as he played the part of an old woman, and created for her a perfect pattern of what the part should be.

The whole company were shown a very old film of *Filumena*, made not long after it was written in about 1946. It is interesting to note that the author, Edouardo di Filippo played the hero himself, although he did not look at all right for the part. Don Domenico was supposed to be a man who had been a real 'lad' in his youth, and who had met Filumena in a brothel. Edouardo di Filippo looked more like an elderly professor. Apparently he had in Naples a little company for which he wrote plays and his sister, a large, florid, blonde blue-eyed Italian woman always played his leading women, so she played Filumena. It would have been difficult to find anyone who looked less like someone who had spent all her early years in a brothel in order to provide for her three sons.

The play is brilliantly constructed, with a dynamic opening scene and a story that builds to an exciting and extremely funny climax. Franco is a fantastic director, inspired and individual, who likes his actors to be creative and at the same time manages to divert them from putting a foot wrong. One day, early in the three-week tour, Franco called my mother to one side and said, 'Patricia, you have two important scenes, and as far as you are concerned they have got to be brilliant. Otherwise it is better to cut them.'

My mother looked him straight in the eye and replied, 'Franco, they *will* be brilliant, but I'm not quite there yet.'

They continued the short tour without Franco, going to Bristol and Bath and on the last night of the tour, just before the opening night in London, the cast were informed that Franco was out front to watch. The show went well, playing to a packed house and, at the end, the cast were asked to remain on stage because Franco wanted to talk to them. Duly he arrived on the stage: 'Well, darlings, I think you've got a big success here. I have just a very few notes for you all.' He looked down at his little note-pad and said, slowly and deliberately, 'Patricia – brilliant!' That was all he said to her. He then went on to give notes to the rest of the company which were all complimentary.

They opened at the Lyric Theatre in Shaftesbury Avenue a few days later and the play was a huge success, running for two years. Joan Plowright headed the company and, since the overall atmosphere always filters down from the top, it was a very happy run for all concerned, though marred towards the end by illness. Joan Plowright developed trouble with her throat which eventually led to her having to rest her voice completely for quite some time. Colin Blakely and my mother were only contracted for eight months and, when they left the play, Joan Plowright was still unwell. The leads in the play were played by their understudies for an almost unprecedented length of time, though eventually a new cast was assembled, this time headed by Barbara Jefford and Frank Finlay.

About a year later my mother received a message that Joan Plowright was going back into *Filumena* for three months; Franco was going to direct it in America, Joan was to be in it, and they were hoping to take my mother with the company. She had never worked in America before and was very keen to go but, unfortunately, American Equity would not allow her to go. (It was not American actors who complained, but English actors who lived in America.) However, she went back into *Filumena* for three more months.

Katharine Hepburn and George Cukor came over to England

in the late 1970s to make a television film of Emlyn Williams'
play, *The Corn is Green*. Out of the blue my mother was
approached to meet them for an interview for the part of Mrs
Wattie.

'I was one of many that they saw,' she recalls. 'I think they
must have interviewed every British character actress over the
age of fifty. They were extremely pleasant to me, and we had
a chat; but I don't think that I was asked to read anything.
Katharine Hepburn asked me if I was Welsh and I told her I
was Irish, and she then said that I reminded her a little of her
mother. I heard nothing more, but a day or two later I was
told that George and Katharine were in the audience of
Filumena. I wondered if they had come to see me work; but,
in truth, they had come to see Colin Blakely – he had recently
appeared in a film with Katharine. After the play was over, I
heard voices coming along the corridor outside the
dressing-rooms. The footsteps came up to my door, but
continued on towards Colin's room. However, one person in
the group did not go past my door. There was a little rap, and
when I opened the door there stood Katharine Hepburn.
"Oh – how lovely to see you! Have you been in front?" I
asked her. "Yes," she replied, "and you were wonderful.
Wonderful – but *what* was that thing on your head?" I told
her that it was a little plait that I had to wear and she said,
"Take it off and refuse to wear it!" She obviously felt that it
was not flattering to my image, and she has a very strong
instinct about image. Ramon Gow, the hairdresser for *The
Corn is Green*, told me that he did everything he could to get
Katharine Hepburn to change her hairstyle in the picture; but
she would not. She always wears that bun – it's her
trademark. The costume designer for the film said to me,
"You have to take Katharine Hepburn on three levels. One is
the person, who is quite wonderful; the second is the star,
who has to pander to her own image, because it is her image
that makes her a star; the third is the film actress, who is
absolutely superb." '

The next day Hazel rang my mother to say that she was

definitely wanted to play Mrs Wattie in *The Corn is Green*. The film was shot in Wales, and is based on Emlyn Williams' own life. It is the story of a young miner whose academic brilliance is recognized by a remarkable schoolteacher who comes to live in the area. She nurtures his talent although a wayward girl, who seduces him and then falls pregnant, almost ruins his chances of a bright future. Katharine Hepburn played the schoolteacher, Toyah Wilcox the young girl, and my mother was her mother. Toyah said that Katharine Hepburn told her that Patricia was the best actress she had seen on any stage. What a wonderful compliment from such a great star!

The location for the film was a farm. The film company erected marquees outside for all the film staff and crew, but Katharine Hepburn had a bedroom allocated to her in the farmhouse where she could change and be made-up. The extremely hospitable people who owned the farm also gave the company a huge room with a great big open fire that was at their disposal when they were not working.

'I came in one day from having done a shot and I think that climbing up into the pony and trap I had caught my foot in my skirt, and the hem was down in the front. As I walked into the room I said to the continuity girl, who was typing away at notes on the previous scene, "I'll have to go out in the rain again and find Wardrobe, because the hem of my skirt is down." Whereupon Katharine Hepburn, who was sitting in the room with Phyllis (her "lady-in-waiting") said, "Phyllis, go upstairs to my bedroom and bring me down that little reticule with my sewing things. I will deal with this. It won't take a minute to sew that hem up here." "Oh, thank you," I said. After a minute or two Phyllis came back, and I held up my hand for the reticule but Katharine Hepburn said, "No, no, no, I am going to sew this up myself." She knelt at my feet and sewed up about ten inches of hem. Later, I said to my dresser, "When you put that garment away after the filming is finished, you should put a label on it: 'Ten inches of the hem on this garment was hand-sewn by Katharine Hepburn!' " I felt very honoured, and it just shows the sort of down-to-earth practical woman that she is.

'Somebody once told me that some friends of theirs broke down in their car outside a house. The car needed water and they were just plucking up the courage to go and ask at the house when a woman came out and asked, "Are you having problems?" "Yes, we need water." "Just wait there." The woman went inside, and came out with water and insisted on pouring it in herself; and they suddenly realized that it was Katharine Hepburn. They thanked her and drove on. Not many big stars would do that.'

My mother thoroughly enjoyed working with Katharine Hepburn. She took her little camera up to Wales and, during the shoot, Katharine turned suddenly towards her when she had her camera poised. My mother asked, 'May I?' and she said, 'Certainly,' and smiled; and my mother took a lovely photo. Katharine kept a copy of the photo. It appeared in her next book, and underneath the photo it says 'Katharine Hepburn – taken by Patricia Hayes.'

13

The National Theatre

The telephone rang one morning in my mother's bright south-facing kitchen; it was William G. Stewart.

'Patricia – it's Bill Stewart here. I'm directing a new series written by Johnny Speight and Ray Galton, "Spooner's Patch". It's a hilarious script – have a look at it; there's a part in it for you. Spooner himself is a villainous policeman in charge of a local police station, a man with no conscience who somehow seems to make a mess of things all the time. During this episode he falls over in the street, getting in the way of a woman who attacks him mercilessly with her umbrella.'

Shortly after she had appeared in her first episode of 'Spooner's Patch' it was decided to change the formula. Johnny Speight spoke to my mother offering to re-write the scripts with her playing Spooner. 'No,' she told him. 'I'm not good when I'm the one in command. I'm at my most funny when I'm rebelling against the one who is in command.'

'I take your point,' said Johnny. 'Let's think about it.' A few days later he rang her again. 'Would you like to play a traffic warden, attached to the police station, in "Spooner's Patch"?'

'Oh, yes,' she said. 'That would just suit me.' She immediately went to the family haidresser, and had her hair dyed red!

Ronald Fraser, who had played Spooner the first time, was not available for the second series. It was not easy to cast Spooner, because he had to be dreadful yet lovable. Donald Churchill was finally cast in the part, and his charismatic personality was just right for the character. My mother played an outrageous traffic warden who was always at cross purposes with Spooner. She was as wicked as he was, but when she was caught red-handed she always managed to gain sympathy by bursting into tears, or using some other form of emotional blackmail.

She loved the part, and the series had all the right ingredients for a big success, but ITV showed the series at the same time as 'Top of the Pops' was shown on BBC – which meant that virtually no young people were watching. 'Spooners Patch' would have appealed to young people because the police, especially Spooner, were always being wrong-footed. 'It was a battle to get my own grandchildren to watch "Spooner", because it clashed with "Top of the Pops". When "Spooner" was over, Katie said to me, slightly accusingly, "I did like 'Spooner's Patch', Granma, and you were very good in it, but I don't know what is top of the pops now. I am completely out of touch with the charts!" It was before the days when everyone had videos, and programmes could be recorded.

'Many things happen behind the scenes in television that the general public are quite unaware of. For example, the big TV companies like the BBC, Thames Television and London Weekend want their shows to have prime-time showing and a small company such as Anglia simply cannot fight with the bigger companies. "Spooner's Patch" did go out during prime time, but "Top of the Pops" was so established and so popular, especially among young people whose lives often revolve around the charts, that it did not stand a chance.

'Sometimes a favourite programme disappears because the TV company that made the show is not strong enough to insist on a prime spot. The larger companies, and the BBC, are in a position to run a new programme until it is successful. It would not be politic to cite examples, but there are quite a few programmes running very successfully now that were considered to be appalling when they were first shown. Equally, the big companies can take off a programme when it suits them, regardless of the following it may have.

'I remember once I had a tradesman putting in central heating for me. He was always prompt and reliable, but one morning he arrived unusually late. When I mentioned it he said, "I was up all night with my wife in hysterics, because the BBC had taken off 'Compact'. She didn't believe that they really would take it off. She sat down to watch it last night at the normal time, and when it did not come on, she suddenly realized that she was never going to see it again. She was in such a state of hysteria that I had to console her. I took her out to supper; eventually I had to get her drunk – ply her with whisky to get her to go to sleep. She was weeping and moaning and saying that she could not bear to think that she was never going to see all those lovely people again. To her, it was like losing a whole family."

'Despite the fact that it was not a huge success, we thoroughly enjoyed making "Spooner's Patch", Bill Stewart is the most delightful and clever man, easy to get on with, and I don't think anyone has ever had more faith in me than he has.'

Later in 1980 my mother starred in a charming play for Yorkshire Television, *Storm in a Broken Teacup*. It was a rather sad story about two lonely people who form a friendship, a proud old lady and a neglected small boy. Hazel rang her when it was over with some exciting news. 'Gillian Diamond, the casting lady from the National Theatre, wants you to go and talk to John Schlesinger about a play that he is putting on there called *True West*, by Sam Shepard.'

She duly went to meet the legendary John Schlesinger, not knowing what to expect. He was very quiet and gentle and the first thing he said was, 'We've met before, you know.'

'Have we?' She could not remember it at all, knowing him only as an extremely famous film director who had directed many films she loved, such as *Darling* (which he himself does not like, but Patricia thought was wonderful and had seen twice.) Eventually she asked him, 'Where have we met?'

'Believe it or not, I tried to be an actor many years ago – and both of us were in a special Sunday show. I remember at the time that you were obviously a very talented young actress, and I was a fairly useless actor.'

'Oh well, the tables have turned now – you are an internationally famous film director, and I am a fairly successful actress,' she said.

'The part that we have you in mind for in *True West* needs to be played with a sort of mid-Southern American accent, we vaguely think it's Tennessee. I have some friends who live in that area, and I've asked them to make a tape for you; you can just listen to these two ladies talking and that will give you a good idea of the accent.'

After her interview with John Schlesinger she went to St Thomas's Hospital to visit Susan Littler, an ex-girlfriend of Richard's. Sue was a most remarkable lady, and an extremely accomplished actress, possibly best remembered as Vivian Nicholson in the BBC production of 'Spend, Spend, Spend', based on the true story of a working-class woman who came from a very harsh background, then suddenly won a fortune on the pools. Poor Susan had been taken ill while working at the National Theatre and rushed to St Thomas's, where a massive malignant tumour was discovered and operated on. She made a temporary recovery – and even worked again – but, sadly, she died a year or so later, a great loss to all who loved her and to the English theatre. After leaving her, my mother went home.

'When I walked in, the phone was ringing. Gillian Diamond had been trying to get hold of me for a couple of hours. "Where have you been? John has been trying to ring you to offer you the part himself. Now he has had to leave for the airport." So I had the part.

'It was my first time at the National, and I liked it very much indeed. Some actors do not like the National, which is

Larking around on the set of 'Spooner's Patch'.
With the late Sidney Bromley in disguise for the film *The Never Ending Story*.

Derek Jacobi, Judy Parfitt and Patricia on the beautiful island of Sark, during the filming of *Mr Pye*.

In the beautiful grounds of the Seigneurie on Sark, 1985.

Richard, Patricia and Teresa after the presentation of Patricia's OBE in 1987.

As the imperious Mrs Cody — the lady with the dogs — in *A Fish Called Wanda*, 1989. (*Georgina Slocombe*).

different from a normal theatre – it is more like going to the office. You have to go through security, then down long corridors to your dressing-room to which you will have a key. Unless you are in more than one play, you will probably be sharing your dressing-room with someone who is in another play on different nights from your own. The woman who was sharing with me always left ours in an awful mess!'

The tape John Schlesinger had lent her became an amusing keepsake – the two women were not involved with the theatre at all. Friends or relations of Schlesinger's, they chattered on, with their slightly drawled Southern accents, about nothing in particular. 'The tape was very helpful to me; I'd agreed to play the part at the National, in the Cottesloe Theatre, with two actors who at the time I knew very little about, Antony Sher and Bob Hoskins. Both of them are now very big stars. *True West* is an excellent play, with an unmistakeable Cain and Abel theme of two brothers, one good, dutiful and hardworking and the other callous, lazy and grasping. The action takes place on the edge of the Mojave Desert, in a house owned by the mother of the two brothers. She has gone away on an extended holiday to Alaska, and the good son is minding the house for her. While she is away the bad son arrives at the house, and by the time she returns a huge fight has erupted between the two brothers, caused entirely by the unbelievable behaviour of the bad son. Her lovely little house has been ransacked and absolutely ruined.

'It was a very strong play, lovely to be in, not too much to learn, brilliant fellow actors and a very good director. John Schlesinger has since asked me to work with him twice; the first time I was not able to because I was already working and the second time he wrote and apologized because he was not going to do the play after all. (A big film had suddenly come up that he had been waiting to do for four years and Peter Hall released him from the National.) John is a marvellous director. I count him among the greats that I have worked with.'

In the light of the variety of roles that my mother has played in her life – girls, boys, witches, tramps, vamps – it is not surprising that the famous Australian Director, Elijah Moshinsky, offered her a part usually played by an old man in his production of *Cymbeline* for BBC Television. 'I know that the soothsayer is always played by a man, but the character is only a sort of fortune-teller who looks into the future and makes prophecies. There is no reason why she should not be an old woman fortune-teller,' he said when he offered her the part.

'Patricia,' said Hazel, that same year, 'Peter Gill, who directed you as Maria in *Twelfth Night*, has been in touch and he wants you to play Rummy Mitchins in his new National Theatre production of Shaw's *Major Barbara*.' My mother accepted without hesitation; she loved working at the National, and she remembered the character of Rummy Mitchins from a production of the play she had seen as a child. She also welcomed another opportunity to work with Peter Gill, and a marvellous cast including Penelope Wilton, Sian Phillips, Brewster Mason and Gillian Martell.

'It was a big cast – only the National and the Royal Shakespeare Company can afford to do plays with those big casts nowadays. They have (or had) the existing back-up staff such as set-builders, electricians, make-up and wardrobe. Actors are very well looked after at the National, waited on hand and foot, treated like Royalty we used to say.'

Johnny Speight rang my mother: 'Pat – I'm writing a series about a woman tramp. She just tramps through life, turning up here, turning up there, living from hand to mouth. Very quick to seize any opportunity that comes her way. I would like you to play her.'

'That sounds wonderful, Johnny. I'd like a companion – another woman coming round with me.'

'Yes, you can have a companion.'

Pat Coombs was cast as the other tramp, and they made a very funny pair because she is very tall and her character was a bit gormless, and my mother was tiny and artful. They lived together in a broken-down old van on a rubbish tip. There was a mattress inside the van, and an old makeshift table outside on which they would make their 'cuppa', using the same tea-bag over and over again. Johnny Speight's scripts were extremely funny. He related a very amusing incident which took place during the making of one of the episodes:

'We had a dwarf on the show, supposed to be a tramp dwarf who lived in a dustbin. In the middle of the scene he takes off the lid and climbs out of the bin and appears to be arguing with a little dwarf wife who is still inside the bin. "Don't start on me – I'll be back when I feel like it," he shouts, and she can be heard screaming abuse at him from inside the dustbin. Eventually he bangs the lid on and storms off, saying, "Bloody women!" to Patricia and Pat Coombs as he goes.

'Our director, Dennis Main Wilson, took the dwarf "to the bank" (to the pub!) with him at lunchtime. They stayed at the bank most of the afternoon. Dennis could handle that bank's hard currency much better than the dwarf could. Someone came to me and said, "Johnny, the dwarf is pissed out of his head." Anyway, it was the day of the show and we had to get on with the take. We were all hoping that everything would be alright. Well – it wasn't. The dwarf stayed in the dustbin when he was supposed to come out, and the other actors had to ad lib around him. Bill Stewart eventually said, "It's no good, we've got to get him out! Come out! You can't go to sleep in there. Get out of the dustbin!" Finally the dwarf tumbled out of the dustbin, knocking it over as he fell. He was shouting abuse at an obviously empty bin and there was a voice answering back, coming from nowhere. The studio audience loved it, they were hysterical at his talking to the empty dustbin. During one take, the dwarf started to make up his own lines. They were pure invention. He also shouted, "Johnny Speight hates dwarfs." We did several takes and managed to struggle through somehow. It was extremely difficult for the other actors not to laugh.'

Another episode in the series had a wealthy drunk end up in the yard where the van parked. He had obviously been to a big party in town, got very drunk, lost his way and ended up in their yard. When the tramps woke up and found him there, they immediately stripped him of anything saleable – his clothes, wallet, gold watch and ring – they even talked about getting all the gold out of his teeth! Finally, they woke him up and told him that he was married to Pat Coombs, that he had gone through a wedding ceremony during the night; and when he wanted to get out of the marriage they demanded money.

A tramp died of a heart-attack in the yard during another episode, and they put him into an old push-chair to get rid of him. As they were wheeling him down the street, people started giving them money; it was the beginning of November, close to Guy Fawkes' Night, and the dead tramp was mistaken for a guy. The tramps suddenly realized that they had a great little business going, and were wondering how long the body would keep, but eventually the police caught them and told them to dispose of their guy. For want of anywhere better to put it, they heaved the body of the dead tramp into the open boot of the police car, shut the lid and a few minutes later the Police car drove away ...

Johnny Speight says: 'I always wondered what happened at the police station a few days later. It would have made a comedy episode in itself! I had visions of people going round sniffing and saying, "There's a nasty smell around here," then eventually finding the decomposing tramp in the boot of the police car. How would they go about investigating that?'

Johnny Speight is fascinated with the whole idea of tramps because, like the Royal Family, they seem to be able to remain right outside the law. He has a theory. 'They are absolutely beyond the law. You can't do anything to them. If you put them in prison, you are probably improving their condition. One of the tramps in the series was complaining about the fact that he could not get into prison and it was coming on towards Christmas. He said, "All me Christmas cards will be in there. I can't stand being outside during the winter months. I've tried everything, but the courts are crowded and they won't hear my case."

'The idea of writing about these tramps came to me one day when I watched a tramp having a pee into a potted plant right outside the smart entrance to Selfridge's Hotel at the back of Oxford Street. Across the street there was a copper watching, who started to walk away as fast as he could. He didn't want to know about it. The commissionaire told the tramp to go away, whereupon the tramp came out with a stream of obscene language. The commissionaire went inside; he didn't want all this language with his guests about. The copper was anxious not to get involved because, if he had arrested him (as he would any respectable citizen) and taken him down to the police station, the sergeant would have said, "Why've you brought him in here? We don't want this bloke stinking the place out. Now we've got to look after him." They'd have had the tramp demanding food and cups of tea. If they hit him, they're in trouble because they can't do that. They might even kill him, they don't know what his health is like. No one in society wants to have anything to do with tramps, and it gives them a certain power.'

'The Lady is a Tramp' was a great success, and was extremely well reviewed by the critics. Channel 4 had only recently started and my mother's series was always high amongst the top ten most popular programmes. After the first series Johnny Speight won the Pye Award for the Best Comedy Scripts, and my mother and Pat Coombs shared the Pye 'Best Actress' Award. Another series was under consideration. Johnny Speight told me: 'Bill Stewart rang me and asked me out to lunch. He said, "Johnny, I don't know how to tell you this. Channel 4 are interested in another series but they'd like to see a trial script!" I said, "we've done a series, and we picked up awards with it, and now they want a trial script! Why don't they just look at what we've done? They can see what it is." Anyhow, I agreed to write a trial script, but half-way through writing it Bill rang me to say that they had decided to go ahead with a new series.'

Though the show had been very successful, as with all Johnny Speight's work it was controversial in various ways.

Channel 4 had probably asked for the trial script in an attempt to make him heed some of their criticisms.

Out of the blue Hazel was contacted by the office of Wolfgang Petersen, the German film director who had directed the award-winning film *Das Bot*. He and Hermann Weigel had written a screenplay for a children's fantasy movie, *The Never Ending Story*, and the person in charge of casting had come to England to find a couple of little elfin people. She hired a studio, videotaped possible actors and actresses as they read excerpts from the script, and sent the videos to Germany – where the decisions were made. My mother and the late Sydney Bromley were chosen to play the quaint little couple, and were immediately flown out to Germany for make-up and costume fittings.

It was to be an American film, made with American money and aimed at the American market, though the text was written by two Germans. The film company decided to film it in Germany, mainly because there are few strikes there (a strike is extremely costly; one can wreck the budget and with it the chances of a movie's success).

Never Ending Story is about a little boy, Bastian, who is going through a very unhappy time. His mother has just died, and he is being bullied by some of the bigger boys at school. Whilst escaping from the bullies on his way to school one day, he runs into an old second-hand bookshop. He leaves there carrying a very strange book which has magical powers; as he reads it, he is transported into a fantasy world filled with weird and wonderful creatures – including a huge white dragon called the Love-dragon. A brave young hero is introduced (obviously Bastian's alter ego) a daring warrior with the tenacity and courage that Bastian has not been able to summon. During the adventures that ensue, among the people who try to help him are an ancient couple. At first sight it is not evident that they are elves but when, later, you see the boy beside them it becomes obvious how tiny they are. My mother was first seen cooking, popping worms into the stew and tasting them: 'Ooh – delicious!' She and Sydney Bromley wore the most elaborate make-ups for their parts as elves, created by an absolute wizard called Colin Arthur.

When my mother realized that she would be living in a hotel in Munich for three weeks during the making of the movie, she contacted her sister Moira, who had spent some time in Germany in her youth, and asked her if she would like to join her for a holiday. Moira who had recently lost her husband, was delighted and off they went together.

'We shared a beautiful twin-bedded room which had facilities for boiling a kettle. Moira took herself off sightseeing every day while I was working at the studios. Her German came back to her quite quickly; when I had free time we would go out together, and Moira could order the meals and hold conversations with people. In fact, I had quite a lot of free time because the animations were so time-consuming. The Bavaria Studios were like enormous aerodrome hangars. The animated Love-dragon was the sole occupant of one of these hangars, and eighteen people were employed to manipulate the head alone. I saw a huge group of people, each of whom was wearing earphones and holding a lead with a little button on the end. Instructions were being passed via the headphones to the operators of the eyelids, nose, mouth, tongue and so on. We were extremely well catered for at the studios; there was a constant buffet where we could help ourselves all day, then at lunch time a huge urn would be brought in with the dish or dishes of the day. They even catered for vegetarians (I've become one, for health reasons).' My mother enjoyed the work, and it was a lovely opportunity for the two sisters to spend some time together. Moira is normally very busy at home, helping her daughter Gina with her seven children!

Another delightful television role was offered to my mother in 1984 in a four-part serial entitled 'Winter Sunlight', by Alma Cullen; it was being made by Limelight Productions for Channel 4, Britain's newest television Channel. Susie

Hush was the producer of 'Winter Sunlight', which
concerned the lives of various older people. The central
figure, played by Elizabeth Sellars, had tolerated a bullying
and negative husband for many years, but tried to make a
break from him at this late stage in her life. My mother
played Alice, a widow, whose family had decided that it was
time for her to go into an old people's home because she
could not manage very well on her own any more. Alice was
not the familiar cockney that my mother so often plays, but
an educated upper-middle-class woman with an arrogant
manner and a proud spirit. There were some hilarious scenes
with Alice misbehaving in the old people's home in a sort of
protest at having been sent there in the first place. Alice felt
degraded at first, but, by the end, she had settled in and was
decorating the Christmas Tree and ordering everybody
about. Another older couple were a sweet-natured man,
played by the late Derek Farr, and his extremely overbearing
wife, brilliantly played by Betty Marsden – she met her
come-uppance when he finally refused to tolerate her
behaviour, and wept to Elizabeth Sellars and my mother in a
very moving scene. It was a delicate subject beautifully
handled by the author, and the scripts were touching and
amusing.

The serial was sensitively directed by Julian Amis. 'A
delightful man,' recalls my mother, 'and an extremely
accomplished director who was on the staff of the BBC for
many years until he retired. Because I was filming *Never
Ending Story*, I joined the others after they had already been
rehearsing for two weeks. The next day Julian Amis wanted
to rehearse a scene between myself and Elizabeth Sellars in
which she came to visit me in the old people's home. I had
learned the lines, they were easy; some lines are easy to learn
and some are difficult. Elizabeth knew her part and we ran
the scene together. Afterwards Julian Amis said, "What a joy
this is – to have two actresses who play so beautifully
together and so effortlessly. Instead of looking at you and
thinking that I've got a lot of work to do, I'm looking at you

and thinking that you are both perfect." Mind you, the script was written by Alma Cullen, and it was a very nice script.'

The director John Gorrie found himself in a predicament just before rehearsals got underway for a new television series, 'Marjorie and Men'. He had engaged Constance Chapman to play Marjorie's mother, but she was involved in a slight car accident. At first the doctors said that she would be well enough to go ahead with the series but, when they realized that she had chipped a piece of bone out of the base of her skull, she had to stay in hospital. Only two days before rehearsals started, John Gorrie sent for my mother. After he had described the part to her she said, 'I don't usually play parts like this.'

'No, you don't. But actors are always complaining; if they play old parts they say that they never get the chance to play young parts; if they play young parts they complain that they never get the chance to play character parts; if it's glamorous parts that they never get the chance to play comedy parts. Here is your chance to play the kind of part you don't normally play!'

'I think I can do it. When I was in Rep, I played everything, but that was many years ago.'

'You'll be perfectly all right. You'll be very good.'

So she accepted the part; but she was a week behind all the others in rehearsal, and it was a struggle for her to get the character right for the first of the series. The narrative involved Marjorie, played by Patricia Routledge, a mature woman who was fancy-free and always hoping to meet Mr Right. Patricia Routledge and my mother worked very well together from the start, with my mother as Marjorie's mum, still interfering in her daughter's life and trying to organize things for her in an annoying, though well-meaning, way.

Marjorie's mother was a very 'smart' woman and, in achieving this, my mother was enormously helped by the make-up artist who looked after her. 'You would not recognize me as Patricia Hayes in some of the photographs from "Marjorie and Men". Lucia Vassallo, who made me up, was absolutely marvellous; she was of Italian extraction and so artistic. The wardrobe department were wonderful too; I was wearing the kind of clothes that I never wear at home. Marjorie is portrayed as a very loving daughter, always kind and sweet to me, but desperately trying to get me off her back. I was always planning things for her and telling her that she would never get a man unless she went about it in the right way. In one episode I brought her some brochures from the Town Hall advertising Old Tyme Dancing. She duly went off to the classes, and it really looked as if she had found Mr Right. Of course, later on in the programme, she discovered that she hadn't. Patricia Routledge and George Baker, who played the possible Mr Right, had to have dancing lessons and they were brilliantly choreographed by Geraldine Stephenson. Marjorie is about forty, has been married before to a man who let her down, and she is a terribly nice person, absolutely straight, very tolerant of her irritating mother and very optimistic even when things fall apart. It was a delightful series; but, after putting all that money into it, Anglia refused to finance another series unless it managed to get prime time, and it did not. I got the part by default, and I thoroughly enjoyed it but another series has never been made.'

14

Sark, *Little Dorrit* & *When We Are Married*

My brother Richard left school at seventeen with very few qualifications because he had sustained serious injuries, one after another, during his final years. He fell and broke his elbow, while standing completely still on the ice-rink at Bayswater. Several operations later it should have been on the mend. However, the plastered arm, set in a right angle, was very heavy; and, in an attempt to rest it, he used to balance his arm on his head. It frequently fell off (nearly wrenching his arm out of its socket) with the result that when the plaster was finally removed, the elbow had not healed at all. It required a metal pin to hold it together! The following year we were returning from holiday in Ireland when he fell off his bicycle on the bridge to the ferry in Rosslare. Somehow, it seems, he managed to scrape up the grey wood from the bridge with his lower teeth and some of it lodged in the floor of his mouth. He was taken to a Welsh hospital, and given penicillin; his mouth healed, but a few weeks later he developed nasty abscesses under his tongue. An exploratory operation at St Thomas's Hospital to discover the reason for the abscesses revealed that he had several huge splinters of wood in the floor of his mouth. Two more operations were required to remove them. He keeps those splinters in a jar to this day.

After leaving school he worked for a while, rather unhappily, as a junior car salesman but eventually he applied to go to drama school. He auditioned successfully for the London Academy of Music and Dramatic Art, and duly completed the course. Equity advised him to change his surname from Brooke because it was too similar to that of some other theatre personalities – Ray Brooks, Richard Broke, Michael Brock and so on – and could have caused confusion. He chose a name from my mother's side of the family, and thus Richard O'Callaghan was born. On leaving LAMDA, Richard went straight into Wedekind's tragic drama *Spring Awakening* at the Royal Court Theatre and from then on he never looked back. He has had a very successful and interesting career with some excellent West End plays to his credit, including *Butley* with Alan Bates and *Three Months Gone* with Diana Dors; he has also worked several times with the Royal Shakespeare Company but, strangely enough, he and my mother had never worked together.

Hazel rang my mother in the spring of 1985. 'Patricia, dear, they are going to send you a script to look at. It's a film script, a film that is going to be made on the Island of Sark and will star Derek Jacobi. It's not a very big part for you but it is rather an amusing character, an Albanian maid. Anyway, dear, they'll be sending you the script and, if you like it, I'll talk money to them. It is not a big budget film, so it won't be a colossal amount.'

'Hazel – look, just ring them and tell them not to bother to send me the script. I don't mind what the money is, I'll take the part!'

'What?' gasped Hazel, unused to such total lack of caution from my mother.

'I don't mind about anything. Just say Patricia says yes to the part, don't bother to send the script.'

'Is that because you want to go to Sark?'

'Yes, of course it's because I want to go to Sark; and I'd like to work with Derek Jacobi.'

'All right, Patricia dear. By the way, the film is called *Mr Pye*, Donald Churchill has adapted the screenplay from the original book by Mervyn Peake.'

Richard rang my mother a few days later. 'Mum – I'm going to be in *Mr Pye* as well! I'm going to Sark for eight weeks; how long are you going to be there?'

'Two weeks.'

Finally, they were going to be working together – and on that strange and beautiful island. That such a tiny island should be so famous is mainly due to the legendary Sibyl Hathaway, Dame of Sark, a most rare woman, who maintained the untouched aspects of the island and at the same time used her considerable charm and influence to draw tourists from all over the world to her jewel in the sea.

'The script arrived, and then a letter from Michael Darwell, the director, asking us to come to a meeting with as many of the cast as possible. I met the producer Judy Marle and also Derek Jacobi, who was to play the strange little man, Mr Pye, and Judy Parfitt who was to play the woman that he stayed with on the island. Richard was cast as an artist who falls madly in love with the island's loose woman, a nympho-maniac, always on the lookout for sailors and possible lovers. He adores her and she is really quite cruel to him. A newcomer, Robin McCaffery, who had never done anything before, was cast as the girl. In some ways it's terrifying to get a big break very early in your career because it's such a let-down if you can't get any work after that. I don't know how she's getting on, I haven't heard from her since. Betty Marsden was also in the cast, and she was marvellous; in my opinion she is a very under-rated actress. My part was Kaka, an Albanian maid who spoke no English at all. It was cod Albanian, all mumbo-jumbo, but written out word for word by Donald Churchill. (Donald is doing much more writing than acting now; he offered me a part in one of his plays recently, but I was busy with *Never Ending Story*.)

'Derek Jacobi's role as Mr Pye was enormous, but Derek knew every word before we started filming. When I asked him how he had managed to learn it all, he explained that he had memorized the whole script initially and then he went over each individual scene the night before we shot it. I never saw him falter! Apart from the fact that he was very good as Mr Pye, he was also lovely to everyone: always polite even when he was not feeling well, always ready to laugh at other people's jokes, always the first to buy a round of drinks. He's an excellent actor and a great catalyst for happiness in a cast. We all had bicycles, and when we went off for a ride it was always Derek who came back to make sure I was all right on the steep parts, patiently waiting behind. He's one in a million.'

Sark is fascinating, and quite unique; one of the few places left on earth where no cars are allowed – which explains why all the cast, including my mother, were riding bicycles. The only motorized transport permitted is a limited number of tractors. They are used to carry furniture and supplies. Five hundred or so people live there, forming a very close-knit community. There are no police and the island is virtually self-governing under a kind of government called the Chief Pleas. It seems to work very well; those who live on the island give the impression that they are extremely happy.

People are attracted to Sark for a variety of reasons. Nature-lovers go because it is noted for its rare wildlife. Historians can discover the remains which indicate that the Romans and the Greeks inhabited the island during their conquests of Europe. There is no airstrip on Sark, the only approach to the island is by ferry from Guernsey. There are two or three ferries daily during the season, and they have to reach Sark at a certain tide in order to dock and unload their passengers safely. It is quite possible to be stranded on Sark because, if the weather is too bad, the ferry will not come.

Apart from a few things, such as the huge aerial mast (presumably for television reception), Sark itself makes you feel as if you are living in the sort of countryside that Shakespeare lived in, because everything is so rampant – nature looking after itself. There are very few roads because they are not needed; there are tracks everywhere that the tractors go along. It is very, very wild and completely safe. Not many of the buildings are new, most of them are old and added to. It would be difficult to get permission to construct a new house there.

Sark came off much better than Guernsey, Jersey or Alderney during the German occupation. The much-maligned Dame of Sark was very persuasive in her arguments with the Germans regarding the way that the island should be managed; she kept her head and appealed to the governing Generals as human beings, and not as enemies. Consequently there was very little destruction or violence on Sark during the War. Very few of the islanders died, just one child who wandered on to a mine field, and a couple who committed suicide rather than be sent to a German detention camp. When the Dame of Sark died, her son, Michael Beaumont, became the twenty-second Seigneur of Sark and inherited the beautiful Seigneurie. My mother was photographed in the grounds of the Seigneurie for publicity during the making of *Mr Pye*.

'Most of the cast were put up in Stock's Hotel. The unit, the management and the producer were at the Hotel Dixcart and the crew spread out in various hotels all over the island. Stock's Hotel was lovely; at first it was quite empty – it must have been May – but a couple of weeks later it was full, and remained so the whole of the time that Richard was there. Richard and I had no scenes together and in fact we were only on the island together for one weekend, then I went home. However, the company asked me to come back, at their expense, for the end-of-picture party, and fortunately I was free and able to go. The only means of transport on the island, apart from bicycles, is horse and cart or tractor. When I was leaving the first time, I got word that the fellow who drove the tractor could attach a trolley to the back for people's luggage; it was very steep between the harbour and the hotel. Normally people would walk along beside the tractor, but the tractor driver said, "I'll be along to pick up

Patricia's luggage and, if she would like, I will borrow an armchair from somebody and she can ride down in the armchair." The woman who ran the hotel later told me, "I saw him driving off with an armchair out of my hotel and I called out, asking him to bring the chair back. I did not realize that it was for you!" '

She had a tremendous send-off, with all the residents following the tractor and taking photographs. Richard, too, was snapping away, and there are even shots of Richard helping her off the tractor and on to the boat.

'We really loved the people of Sark – they were gorgeous, absolutely gorgeous. One day word went round that there was to be a stunt, and that anybody who wanted could come and watch from the far side of the harbour (a device had been built, for the stunt, on the near side). A horse was to seem to go over the cliff on a very narrow part of the island, called "La Coupée"; it is so narrow that normally not even a horse and cart is allowed to go along it. Everybody gathered – lots and lots of people; the stuntman was all dressed up in Derek Jacobi's costume with great big white wings, because Mr Pye is supposed to be so good that he sprouts wings – and when the islanders chase him over the cliff he is able to fly. We were all sitting on the cliff, waiting for the stunt to be performed, when I noticed a small boy sitting right on the edge, just where the cliff sloped away rather dangerously. One of the Sark women said to me "Oh that boy – I'm going mad! Any minute now he'll be over the side of the cliff, and down there!" she pointed to the abyss. "Well," I said, "it's not quite a sheer face. He'll probably be all right. Is he yours?" "No." "Do you know whose he is?" "We're all aunties. If you're not someone's mother here, you are their aunt – and I can't bear to see him. I've known him and all his brothers and sisters since they were born." Fortunately, nothing did happen to the boy, although the stuntman himself was slightly injured shortly afterwards.'

After the end-of-picture party, as Richard and Mum were sitting in the ferry awaiting its departure, the owner of

Stock's Hotel came rushing down to the harbour, waving a little English flag and shouting, 'I simply couldn't let you go without coming to wave you goodbye!'

The BBC decided to put on a series of four Noël Coward short stories, adapted for television by well-known writers. Out of the blue my mother was contacted by the producer Alan Shallcross, regarding one of the four plays called 'Mrs Capper's Birthday', for which the script had been written by Jack Rosenthal.

'I went up to see them at the BBC. There were several people in the office including Alan Shallcross, Jack Rosenthal and the director, Mike Ockrent, who had just had an enormous success with his production of *Me and My Girl* at the Victoria Palace Theatre. I read a little of the script for them, and they thanked me for coming, but I really had no idea whether they had liked me or not. However, the next day the telephone rang, and they offered me the part. Jack Rosenthal had adapted "Mrs Capper's Birthday" extremely well, and it was a really lovely role for me.'

Mrs Capper is a charming older lady who earns herself some pocket-money by doing a little washing-up and cleaning for people. Her much-loved husband, Fred, was killed during the Second World War, but she still continues a very lively relationship with him in her mind, chattering away to him all day. The action takes place in 1972, but to her Fred is still the young man whom she married all those years ago. Hilda Capper lodges with a friend, Alice, who is not a particularly happy woman and takes it out on Hilda. However it is difficult to get the better of someone who is so basically good-natured, and Hilda seems to come out on top in the end.

The play opens with Hilda Capper wishing 'Good morning' to a black and white photo of Fred, in his army uniform, which sits in a frame on the table beside her bed. After a chat to Fred, she gets dressed and goes downstairs, where Alice gives her a birthday present. Even then, Alice finds it impossible to be pleasant to Hilda; she obviously envies her her happy nature.

Hilda sets off to her Sunday morning job, washing-up for some Yuppies who live in Westminster. There has been an enormous dinner party the night before, and the kitchen is a chaotic mess, with lots of dirty dishes and dozens of empty bottles. Mrs Capper raises her eybrows good-naturedly and sets about the task of clearing the dishes. Meanwhile, upstairs, the lady of the house, Mrs Nash, wakes up with a colossal hangover to discover to her horror that she is in bed not with her husband, but with one of the other dinner guests. Mr Nash has also awoken; on discovering that he is in the home and bed of another of the dinner guests, he telephones home and asks Mrs Capper to tell his wife not to worry, that he will be home soon, that he can explain everything and that nothing happened! Having taken the call and the message, Mrs Capper is understandably rather bemused and amused when her mistress comes downstairs and asks for a cup of coffee for herself and her husband. In all the confusion that follows, Mrs Capper and Mrs Nash become allies against the men, and out of gratitude she is given a very nice Victorian brooch for her birthday.

Later in the day she has to be very diplomatic when she receives a present and a proposal of marriage from Alice's gentleman friend. Alice assumes, quite wrongly, that Hilda has been carrying on with her beau and loses no opportunity of trying to spoil the evening when they are all taken out to dinner by Mrs Capper's daughter and son-in-law. Despite a few hiccoughs, Mrs Capper has a wonderful birthday and ends the day as she began it, lying in bed chatting away to her Fred. It is a simple and very charming story, and was delightfully directed by Mike Ockrent and extremely well acted by all concerned.

'Kathryn Pogson played Mrs Nash who employed me, she is a very busy and gifted actress and we thoroughly enjoyed our scenes together. Avis Bunnage, a very good character actress, was the sour Alice. Paula Wilcox played my daughter, she was so good and so lovely to work with. I almost felt that she *was* my daughter. Gary Waldhorn acted her rather belligerent husband superbly, and the one and only Max Wall played Avis Bunnage's supposed suitor. I based my character on Mrs Stillwell (Nan Nan), my "mother's help" for years and years and years, whom I've already mentioned earlier.

'When you are playing an important part, the BBC really looks after you. A beautiful wig was made for me, one of the best I've had. Wigs, make-up and clothes are terribly important because if they don't match up with the character that you are creating, you will never be happy in the part. You will say, "Yes, it's a lovely part – but I'm wrong in the dress." The wardrobe mistress for "Mrs Capper", Rita Reekie, was wonderful. The clothes were absolutely right; we tried on and tried on and tried on and eventually she said to me, "Yes." And I said, "Yes." Very few people outside the profession know what a difference the costume makes to an actor. Beryl Reid always talks about the feet being first; she builds her costume from the feet upwards. The designer can create an impression of what the character needs, but that has got to fit in with the actor or actress who is actually playing the part. In my early days in repertory I just had to make the most of whatever was chosen and sent down from the costume hire shop. It is not until you start to work in high-quality productions that you realize why designers are paid a lot of money to make things look and feel right. I remember when the musical *My Fair Lady* opened in London, the public were staggered by the costumes. All of a sudden these frightfully expensive and gorgeous costumes were on the stage. All through the war everything had had to be as cheap as possible, and in any case it was impossible to buy the materials; and before the War Productions were not quite so ambitious. Nowadays people spend the earth on costumes and scenery; and in my opinion it is well worth it.'

Hazel rang 'Patricia dear' yet again, and said, 'Richard Goodwin, who picked up a lot of awards with his production of *A*

Passage To India, is doing a screen version of *Little Dorrit* and they are going to send you a script with a view to playing the part of Affery.'

When she first read the script she was not sure whether she wanted to play Affery. There were other women's parts, more dramatic or funnier, that she preferred. Hazel reported back to Sands Films who were producing it: 'Patricia says she would love to be in the film; but she would really like a more interesting part.' She was told that Christine Edzard, the director and writer of the screenplay, had had my mother in mind for the part of Affery for the past two years. She read the script again, and decided to accept the role.

'I realized it was a more meaningful part than some of the others. In a sense, Affery haunts the Clennam household because she has always been there in the background of Arthur Clennam's life. When he was a little boy, and Mrs Clennam was so cruel to him for reasons that she thought were right, Affery was the one who really mothered him. As the film progresses you realize why Mrs Clennam was as she was. Her husband had had an affair, and Arthur was the child of that union. Mrs Clennam made things very difficult for them, hounding her husband's mistress to her death; she was totally unforgiving and never forgave the fact that her husband had broken his marriage vows. On the death of Arthur's mother, she takes the boy in and brings him up – but she always resents him.

'It was filmed in the studios built by and belonging to Sands Films at Rotherhithe, right on the Thames. With the redevelopment of London's Docklands, Sands Films got in very early and bought a huge warehouse site. Richard Goodwin, who owns Sands Films, is married to Christine Edzard, the director of *Little Dorrit*, and they have an apartment at the warehouse in Rotherhithe. They are wonderful people to work for. Everyone connected with the film was thrilled and happy doing it. The wardrobe department worked for weeks and weeks before the filming started; every single costume was hand-made. There was an exhibition of all the costumes at the London Museum timed to coincide with the release of the film, an opportunity for the public to see for themselves the care and detail that had gone into the making of these exact copies of the clothes of Dickens's era. All the scenery was made and erected on the premises. Everything was shot at Rotherhithe; the fronts of the houses were only façades, the inside rooms were built separately. If you have the space to build sets, it is much cheaper than sending people out on location – and they have heaps of space there. However, they only tackle one film at a time and they wait to see the outcome before they plan the next.

'There was a magnificent cast. Alec Guinness was William Dorrit, Little Dorrit's father, a wonderful part and he was brilliant in it. However, on this occasion we did not meet; Affery does not cross his path at all. Cyril Cusack, one of Britain's finest character actors, played his brother, Frederick Dorrit. Joan Greenwood was Mrs Clennam; sadly, she died before the film was released. The late Bill Fraser played Mr Casby and we were destined to work together yet again soon afterwards. Derek Jacobi excelled himself as the hero once more, but Arthur Clennam was a serious character – unlike Mr Pye, who was a caricature. Miriam Margolyes, an extremely expert and very clever actress, played Flora. Max Wall, who had proposed to me in "Mrs Capper's Birthday", played my husband Flintwinch, and once again he gave a remarkable performance.

'Joan Greenwood and I used to be collected in the same car, because we both lived on the same side of London. I had never met her before, but I grew to like her enormously. She was gorgeous to work with and she had so much humility, sincerity and love. She was married rather late in life to André Morrell, an actor who made a big name for himself when he starred in an early television science-fiction thriller called "The Quatermass Experiment". She lived in Fulham with her son, who was still at university when I met her; unfortunately she had already lost her husband. We used to call for her and take her to the studios. She was not very strong, and during the breaks she would be quietly resting in her dressing-room, while I would be tearing about in my usual way. People always ask me where I get my enormous vitality from and I say, "I don't know where I get it from, but my father had it and my ex-husband had it. It is something that you are born with. I used to think that I would never find any man to keep up with my boundless energy until I met my husband. He had even more energy than I had."

'Christine Edzard was tremendous to work with, an extremely discerning director, and we were looked after very, very well. It was another extremely happy episode in my career.'

Before *Little Dorrit* was released, someone from the Theatre of Comedy rang Hazel and said, 'We are putting on *When We Are Married*, and we'd like Patricia to play Mrs Northrop. If she is interested, please ask her to make an appointment to go and see Ron Eyre who will be directing.'

My mother recalls: 'I made an appointment to see Ronald Eyre at his home the following Tuesday. We spoke about things in general, and the part in particular, for three and a half or four hours. Remembering the times we had shared during *Habeas Corpus*, I told him how I'd waited and waited for him to tell me I was good as Mrs Swab, and how in the end I'd dragged it out of him. We talked about the problems each of us had had with Alan Bennett's brilliant, but very difficult, script. Very often in the profession, because of the problems each individual is experiencing, you leave the play feeling that you did not think very much of someone or that they did not appreciate you. Years later you meet again, in something quite different and, because you have that previous experience in common, without all the associated stresses, you begin talking to each other and you soon discover that in fact you really relate extremely well and your attitude towards one another alters. Also people *do* change as they gain experience, and of course, we mellow over the years. When I was struggling along in *Habeas Corpus* it must have seemed to Ron Eyre and Alec Guinness that I was some awful, depressed, humourless creature. When I am in a show where I am happy, people think of me as full of fun and ready for mischief.'

Ron Eyre asked my mother how she felt about playing Mrs Northrop: 'You see, I want to assemble the perfect cast.'

'I was once asked to play Mrs Northrop before, and – for some reason – I was unable to do it. Afterwards I was glad, because when I was in the play years ago, playing Ruby Birtle, I did not think very much of the character. She has one or two good lines; but she was a moaner.'

'She shouldn't be. She is exactly like one of my aunties – she just walks straight in and says what she thinks. She kowtows to nobody. She is not a conceited person, but it does not matter how grand a person is, she will not let them lord it over her. When Mrs Northrop comes to do a day's charring for the three women, on this big occasion of their silver wedding anniversary, she has no respect at all for the airs and graces that they give themselves. In the end, she reminds them that she used to know them when one of them was weighing apples and potatoes in the family greengrocer's shop. She shrieks laughing when she discovers that they are not really married.'

My mother decided to play the part. Ron Eyre told each member of the cast who would be playing the other parts; he told my mother that her fellow actors would include Elizabeth Spriggs, Timothy West, Prunella Scales, Bill Fraser, Patricia Routledge, James Grout and Brian Murphy. 'As for the part that you once played, Patricia, Ruby Birtle, I've seen a girl. This is how it came about. A young north-country girl was recommended to me; she came down for an interview and we talked about the play but, when I asked if she would like to be in it, she said that she wasn't able to because she was making a film! I asked her why she had come all that way to talk to me about a play that she could not do, she replied, "Well I wanted to meet you." ' Luckily for her, Ron Eyre is not an aggressive person and he understood her reason.

'Well now, in that case,' he said, 'can you think of anybody who could play the part really well?'

'Yes,' said the girl. 'There's an actress called Sue Devaney.'

'How will I get hold of her?'

'She's doing Pantomime in Bolton.'

So he sent for Sue Devaney, she travelled down from Bolton in the morning and hurried back that afternoon for the performance. Ron Eyre was very impressed with her composure from the minute she walked into his apartment. She was not at all overawed by him or his artistic and cultured surroundings. She read beautifully and he gave her the part.

'He made a very good choice' says my mother 'because she was marvellous in the part and she's an absolutely darling girl.

'Ron Eyre told me that the Theatre of Comedy approached him to produce *When We Are Married*, and he told them that it was his favourite of all Priestley's plays, his masterpiece. However he had stipulated that he would only direct it for them if they would let him cast every single person perfectly. The Theatre of Comedy told him to go ahead and do what he liked. We must have been a very expensive cast, none of us was cheap!'

My mother thoroughly enjoyed the part of Mrs Northrop under the direction of Ron Eyre and, from the very first performance of *When We Are Married* until the last, they played to packed houses. They also made some much-needed money for the Theatre of Comedy.

The Whitehall Theatre was the perfect venue from the point of view of the stage. They had a beautifully designed set, and the lighting and the costumes were second to none. However, backstage there was very little room for such a large cast. Most theatres have a divan in each dressing-room, but those at the Whitehall are very small, and the women's costumes were elaborate, with corsets and numerous petticoats. Apparently Timothy West and Prunella Scales, who are married to each other, shared a dressing-room, and if Prunella wanted to have a rest between shows on days when they had a matinée, Timothy West had to leave the room so that she could stretch out on the floor!

Some time in the first six months of *When We Are Married*, Hazel rang my mother to tell her that Peter James had approached her regarding a new play that was to have a limited season at the Lyric Theatre, Hammersmith. He was putting on, and the great Spanish director, Nuria Espert, would direct, Lorca's *The House of Bernarda Alba*. Hazel was not very enthusiastic because the part seemed small. Meanwhile, the cast of *When We Are Married* were encouraging my mother to stay on after her six-month contract had expired.

The script arrived and, having read it, she decided that she could not make head nor tail of it anyhow. 'Hazel – thank Peter James for asking me to be in *The House of Bernarda Alba*, but tell him that if I am to go to the Lyric, Hammersmith, it will have to be a much better part.'

However, a week later she received a letter from Peter James: 'Please – please – think again. I've never thought of Maria Josepha as a small part, it is so perfectly placed in the play. I cannot think of anybody who would play it better than you would.'

'Hazel – Peter James has written and asked me to think again.'

'Yes, dear – and they've now told me something they didn't tell me before. Glenda Jackson and Joan Plowright are both going to be in it!'

'I cannot turn down a play that has both Glenda Jackson and Joan Plowright in it! They are not fools, they will only be in a play if it is really worth doing.'

'Yes, I think you must do it, dear – it's just that there seemed to be so few lines in it for you when I first read it.'

Both my mother and Hazel had found the original translation rather laboured but there was a new text on its way. Once my mother had accepted the role of Maria Josepha, Peter James brought Nuria Espert to see her in *When We Are Married*, at the Whitehall Theatre. Although

Mrs Northrop was an entirely different character from Maria Josepha, Nuria Espert could see the quality of my mother's performance – she was delighted to have her to direct in *The House of Bernarda Alba*.

Federico García Lorca, who wrote *The House of Bernarda Alba*, was one of Spain's great poets and playwrights. His dramatic works are full of poetry and beautiful to listen to, particularly in the original Spanish. *The House of Bernarda Alba* was one of his last works; shortly after its creation, he was killed, shot at night without trial by the Nationalists in Granada at the outbreak of the Spanish Civil War. One possible reason was that he was a very famous figure, who came from an 'establishment' family; another that he was suspected by some of being a homosexual. He certainly had no political ambitions whatsoever and was always on the side of the oppressed and downtrodden. His death was a tragic loss to Spain's literature, and it shocked the whole of Europe and America.

15

Bernarda Alba
& the OBE

Work began on *The House of Bernarda Alba*. Nuria Espert endeared herself enormously to the cast because she had a great knowledge of Lorca, was very truthful and extremely encouraging. They blossomed under her loving and appreciative eye. 'When asked how I got on with Nuria, I would say "famously". Every time we rehearsed, and I made alterations as the part grew, she would say in her warm Spanish accent, "Patricia you are wonderful!" Actors find it very encouraging to be thrown bouquets by their directors.'

The play is profoundly Spanish in essence. The action all takes place during a swelteringly hot summer. Bernarda Alba, a Spanish matriarch, has managed to keep her five daughters unmarried and to herself, by enforcing the strict traditions of the period and preventing them from going out. The plot begins just after the death of Bernarda's husband. The eldest daughter is about to inherit money, and therefore – although physically plain and delicate and approaching forty – she has become an attractive proposition to one of the local men, years younger than herself, who is intending to marry her. The arrival of a young, handsome, virile male among all those frustrated females in the family causes havoc, even though we, the audience, never actually get to see him. A tragic ending is inevitable.

195

Maria Josepha, Bernarda's mother, is eighty, and is kept locked away most of the time because she is senile and an embarrassment to the rest of the family. At dead of night she steals out of her room into the main house, and the script states that she is carrying a lamb.

'Nuria – what do you think about the lamb?' asked my mother.

'Well, the lamb is nothing. It can be a piece of cloth.'

'You mean like a child's comforter, that has to go to bed with him night after night?'

'Yes – like that.'

'Afterwards,' says my mother, 'I had the idea that the lamb could be a home-made toy that had once belonged to one of her grandchildren. When I went to have my costume fitted by the Lyric Theatre's wonderful wardrobe lady, I said to her, "I don't know what I'm going to do about the lamb. I see myself as having a piece of sheepskin, made to look like a lamb but with all the stuffing taken out so that it is bedraggled and old." "Wait a minute," she said excitedly and she got her step-ladder, climbed up it and reached to a very high-up cupboard and flipped something out with her finger. It was a toy lamb. "There it is, Pat – it's been waiting for you all this time." So they pulled the stuffing out, leaving his lamb's face, his body and his little legs. I became devoted to that darling lamb; I loved it, it was like a part of me.'

Nuria was unable to attended rehearsal one day and Glenda Jackson took over. They were rehearsing a scene in the last act in which the whole house is quiet and everyone asleep. Suddenly the door opens and the ghostly figure of Maria Josepha appears, just draped in an old veil – very see-through. She is carrying the toy lamb. Probably when it was first performed in Spain, where they have access to lambs, it would have been a little new-born lamb, something that Lorca (who had spent most of his childhood on a farm) would have found completely natural. Maria Josepha's lines are: 'Little lambkin child of mine, we shall walk down to the edge of the shore. The little ant will stand at his door, you shall have bread and take my milk.'

Glenda said, 'I think, at that point, you should put the lamb to your breast and feed it.'

'Put it to my breast! You don't really think I should?' My mother felt quite horrified.

'Yes, I do. That's what she says: "You shall have bread and take my milk".' replied Glenda, in a matter-of-fact tone.

My mother, who had fed her own three children (and one other baby!) decided to put aside her own feelings and do exactly as Glenda suggested. From then on she always put the toy lamb to her breast. Nuria had not suggested it, but when she returned the next day, and after my mother had completed the scene, her reaction was: 'Patricia you are wonderful!' Later, someone sent my mother a postcard of a Chilean woman feeding a lamb. Apparently, because the farmers were poor, and could not afford to lose any stock, if they had the misfortune to have a ewe die, and there was not another to foster its lamb, a nursing mother might be asked to feed it herself.

The play was an enormous success and my mother was extremely grateful to Peter James for persuading her to take the part when she originally turned it down, instead of just offering it to someone else. It is always inspiring to work with a brilliant cast. Dressing-room space is limited at the Lyric, Hammersmith, so Joan Plowright and Glenda Jackson agreed to share; and my mother also shared, but stipulated that it should only be with a non-smoker. 'They put me in with Gillian Hanna, who was playing the maid, and from the moment we met, up until now, we've been the greatest of friends. We never stopped laughing. Glenda and Joan often made remarks about the amount of noise that came from our room.

'Joan Plowright was her usual gracious and charming self, as pleasant and appreciative as she had always been. By then we had in common that my son and her daughter had both been at Chichester the year before. I used to ask her questions about Tamsin, and realized from her replies that even the daughter of Sir Lawrence Olivier and Joan Plowright has to make her own way, and face up to the competition, like any other young actress.

'Glenda Jackson is a remarkable woman – she led us to victory. She has qualities of leadership without being at all bossy, and she always knows exactly what she wants. She would make a wonderful director if she could fit it into her enormously heavy schedule. I never got to know her as a person; but she hates praise of any kind and is not interested in curtain calls! At the end of the play the whole cast made a line right across the stage: the curtain would go up, and we would bow, and then it would come down – and that was all. There was a standing ovation nearly every night, and I felt that the audience wanted more than that. It was no good saying to Glenda, "Why don't you take a call on your own?" I knew that she would not wear that! One day I said to Glenda, "I think the curtain calls are too quick." She replied, "They can't be quick enough for me!" I started to say, "I think the curtain should go up ..." but Glenda interrupted me. "Let's all listen to what Madame has to say about the curtain calls. Yes, Mother – how should the curtain calls be done?" I told her and everyone else how I felt the call should be given, so that the audience would not feel cheated. I could see Joan Plowright laughing, but I think she agreed with me – and we did change the call. Even then, Glenda would often be caught walking off the stage as the curtain rose for another call, and she would turn to me with mock annoyance and say, "You and your curtain calls!" All that Glenda wanted to do at the end of the show was to rush home to her seventeen-year-old son; and I can well appreciate that, having done the same thing myself for so many years.'

The play was originally intended to transfer to the West End if it was successful. The run at the Lyric was extended by three weeks, while a suitable West End theatre was sought. When Gillian Hanna was asked if she wanted to transfer, she told the management that she didn't really want to transfer in such a small part, but 'I am willing to do so on condition that

I can still share a dressing-room with Patricia!' The feeling was completely mutual.

When the play was about to come off at the Lyric, and it was still not certain that there was a theatre to go to, my mother was suddenly asked if she would like to go to Birmingham to see Robin Midgely at the BBC about a television play.

'I went off to Birmingham to meet Robin Midgely, a very well-known television director; and at the same time I met Heidi Thomas, the young girl who had written the play. When Heidi Thomas walked in I could not believe that she was the author – she looked about eighteen! (In fact she was twenty-two)

'The play was *Our Lady Blue* and it was about a home for destitute women, in a convent. The home was run by a few nuns, the Mother Superior being superbly played by Doreen Mantle. I was to play a Liverpool Irish ex-prostitute who had been on the game for years, but was now down-and-out and old and pathetic. She can spend every night at the home but she is not allowed in before 6 p.m. The reason for the title *Our Lady Blue* is that one day, when she was having one of her tantrums – she was a naughty old thing – she picked up a paintbrush that was being used by one of the young voluntary helpers and daubed the paint everywhere. He had been painting the statue of the Virgin Mary with blue paint. Later, while washing it off her hands, she says, "That is Our Lady blue. I had a dress in Our Lady blue once."

'A couple of young people helping at the home take pity on the pathetic creature, who is obviously dying of VD, and when the Mother Superior refuses to arrange for her to go on a trip to Lourdes they plan a mock-up trip. They wake the old girl up, and tell her that she is going to Lourdes. She is placed in a wheelchair, wrapped in blankets and taken on an imaginary boat ride in a darkened cellar, with the sounds of seagulls and the noise of the sea. Eventually they reach the chapel where a black boy has put a crown of candles on the Virgin Mary. They have also rigged up a children's paddling pool in front of the statue. When they wheel her in to the candle-enclustered chapel she really thinks that she is at Lourdes: there is the Virgin Mary in a halo of candlelight and the air is filled with the sounds of her favourite Mario Lanza record, "Be My Love". At a given moment the young people lead her gently to the paddling pool; she kicks off her slippers and steps into it, and they lower her deep into the blessed water. Suddenly, the lights come full on – and into the hardly recognizable chapel comes the Mother Superior. She is furious!

'Heidi Thomas, who wrote the play, is now resident playwright at the Liverpool Theatre. She has already had a play put on at The Other Place at Stratford. She is an extremely clever and charming girl with an amazing gift for such a young age. I loved being in her play, I really did.'

Bernarda Alba, re-opened at the Globe Theatre as soon as my mother returned from Liverpool; and it was just as big a success as it had been at the Lyric, Hammersmith. It had a limited run of three months, which was then extended to five months. During the run, Noël Davis, who was involved in the casting of George Lucas's new movie, *Willow*, came to see the play. Shortly afterwards she received a call telling her that a car would come to fetch her to take her to Elstree, where they would like to see her for a part in *Willow*.

'When I arrived there I did not actually see George Lucas – I was ushered into a big room where I was interviewed by Ron Howard, the director. I noticed that my interview was being rather discreetly videoed. Ron Howard chatted to me about what I had done and then he described the part to me. There are two witches in *Willow*; basically one is a good witch and the other is evil. Mine was the good witch, Raziel. When you first meet her she is under an evil spell placed on her by Bavmorda, the wicked witch, and she has been changed into a little furry animal; then she is tranformed from a furry animal into a big bird, then she becomes a goat, but finally the magic spell is found that can turn her back into the woman she once was. However, she is now an older version of the beautiful woman she used to be because the years have gone by. A tremendous battle between the two witches ensues.

'Jean Marsh played Bavmorda – I had never met her before – and what fun we had. We also went through torture some of the time! What no one had told us was that the whole of the battle between the two witches would take place indoors – but in the Queen's Tower, which was open to the sky, in the pouring rain. I implored Ron Howard, "Can't we have that lovely fine spray, like the gentle rain that they have in Ireland?" He replied, "No, unfortunately you can't. That wouldn't show up on the film. Torrential water on film looks wonderful, a little soft spray looks nothing." So we had to bear it. Our beautiful wigs were drenched. The wig mistress said, "If only I had known!" She had ordered the most beautiful fine hair for the wigs. Luckily, she had ordered two for me; so when I did eventually appear high and dry I still had a good wig. I was glad that both the wigs were good because although it was fine hair it used to build up into a sort of bubble at the back of my neck that was very uncomfortable. Every now and then I would say, "Look – I've had enough – I've got to get everything wet off and be dried out and warmed through. If I continue like this I'll be ill." I don't know how Jean Marsh managed, because after the first two or three days in which we worked together, they proceeded to do all her scenes. When I met her later she said, "It has been hell this week – absolute hell. All that I could do was bear it and think of the money!"

'I did not meet the producer, George Lucas, until we were on the set. He leaves everything to Ron Howard, with whom he has been working for a long time. I imagined that George Lucas would be a big guy with one of those ten-gallon Stetson hats, very American, middle-aged and dressed in expensive and very showy clothes. I don't know why I thought that. One day when we were on the set I asked someone, "Is George Lucas here today?" "Yes." "Where?" "Over there." "Do you mean that man in the jeans?" I was amazed when I saw him. He looked like a librarian, interesting and clever but not at all opulent. However, he becomes dynamic when he is working.

'The hero in *Willow* is played by a dwarf called Warwick Davis. When George Lucas enquired whether I liked the movie, I replied that the thing I most liked about it was that the hero was a dwarf. George Lucas smiled and said, "Well I've used these little people in many of my films – but they've nearly always been inside bits of machinery, or they've been microbes, or science fiction people. I used to see them around the studio and think that I would like to make a film about one of them. They are just the same as you or me, but they happen to be very small of stature. I thought, why can't one of them be the hero? I've had my eye on Warwick for some time because he's got a lovely face. He's no fool; in fact, he's very clever and he's a good actor. Ron Howard and I have been inventing this story and working on it with a writer for about two or three years."

'George Lucas told me that he been accused of overspending in his movies so one of the other producers, called Nigel Wool, had the special assignment of constantly cheese-paring. It was not an enviable task or a popular appointment. For example, he would appear in the make-up room, making sure that they really needed the extra make-up artist who had been hired for that day. I used to feel sorry for Nigel.

'I throughly enjoyed my sessions in the make-up room. The head of make-up was Alan Boyle and his female assistant was called Tommy. They had frequently worked together; sometimes she had been the boss and he had been her assistant. They knew each other really well and there was a constant stream of amusing badinage between the two of them. My make-up was not complicated, but I did have to have a mask made of my face. It was for my stunt double who was doing the fight scenes, which were too dangerous for me to do myself. My double was called Ellie, and she was about my height and build. When they make the mask you have to sit up and they put this plastic stuff (the same plastic dentists use to make a mould for false teeth) all over your face, quickly making pencil-size holes for your nose and mouth so that you can breathe, then you have to sit still for about ten minutes. The next time I was in the room I asked, "What is that thing there?" "That is you – that is your face." "That's not my face." "It is – it is your mask." "But it's dreadful!" While the mask is drying on your face it must gradually slide down – the mouth was turned down, the nose was down, everything was down.

'We did the scenes a few days later, and Ron Howard said to me, "Now we are picking it up from where Bavmorda has thrown this thing at you, and hurled you against the spikes, and you have dropped down on the ground. We will show you the stunt-double doing it on the video." I saw this girl fighting and battling and then Bavmorda hurled her to the ground. She looked quite like me in the mask; but me at my worst, it was very depressing! Everybody hates it and make-up artists are generally told not to let the actors see their own masks. The stunt girls were very experienced, they knew exactly where to put the protective padding without it showing.

'I had one particular scene with Warwick Davis near the end of the film, when Willow and Raziel were approaching the castle of the wicked witch Bavmorda. We could see the battlements and the enormous guards standing on them in full armour. I shouted, "We call upon you to surrender!" Whereupon there were shrieks of laughter from the men on the battlements. Then we began to advance. At that point Ron Howard, the director, said, "Cut – that's fine. Now, Patricia, I want you and Warwick to stand there, say that line again, hear the laughter, then you will see the drawbridge open – it comes down with quite a bang, and the moment it's down six horsemen will come out of the castle and advance towards you over the plain." I had seen these horsemen rehearsing in their marvellous old-fashioned suits of armour. "These horses and their riders are part of Bavmorda's army and they will eventually fight with your army, who are hidden. I want a shot of the drawbridge coming down and these men on horseback advancing towards you and Willow." (The distance between where we stood and the drawbridge was about fifty yards.) "It will look as if they are going to come right on top of you but they won't. They will pull up a good ten yards before they get to you."

'Ron Howard said, "Action!" I said, "We call upon you to surrender." The laughter. The drawbridge began to move and crashed down with a resounding *bang*! Immediately there was the noise of the hooves on the wood. The six gigantic horses came thundering towards us, tearing across the plain at full speed – the knights with their helmets and their spears and the horses charging and leaping forward. They reached a point about twelve yards from us, and I could see the riders pulling them up – within ten yards from us they had stopped. Except for one – the one on the outside – the one facing me! The rider could not stop it, and I could see it was coming on. I thought to myself, "What shall I do?" In a split second I decided to stand my ground. If I had run he might have pulled it on to me. About two yards from me the rider managed to turn the horse's head and the animal went round in a circle, then stopped. I turned round to the cameras as if to say, "What's this – you said it was going to stop!" Everybody was absolutely silent for a moment and then people started rushing over to me to see if I was all right. Willow, who had darted away when he saw what was happening, said to me, "My goodness – you were brave." I said, "I wasn't brave – I was just convinced that the horse would not trample me. It's not in their nature."

'Apparently, while they were watching the day's rushes that evening, George Lucas remarked to Ron Howard, "Did you see Pat's face at the end of that shot? Did you see the expression on her face?" '

After *Willow* had been filmed my mother appeared in two hilariously funny episodes of 'In Sickness and in Health', the follow-up to 'Till Death Us Do Part'. Johnny Speight wrote some scripts which included both Irene Handl and my mother. Warren Mitchell says that he really enjoyed those episodes because they gave him a break; normally he is talking nearly all the way through the programme which must be unbelievably strenuous.

Priscilla John contacted Hazel later that year telling her that she was casting a film for John Cleese: *A Fish Called Wanda*. There was a part in it suitable for my mother. Hazel telephoned her: 'Patricia, dear, I've received the script for *A Fish Called Wanda*. There are only about four lines for you. I don't know if you will want to do it.'

'Well, yes, I do. I don't care how many or how few lines there are – I'd like to be in anything John Cleese is doing.'

Apparently, when my mother was suggested for the part, John Cleese was not certain that she would be ideal because he had seen her in so many cockney parts and Mrs Cody was rather upper-class. He decided to interview her. My mother went off to meet John Cleese, all prepared to convince him that she could play an up-market character. However, all he said to her was, 'How are you with dogs?'

'You won't find anyone better!' she was able to reply, with conviction.

'How so?'

'I love dogs – I've had dogs in my life all my life. I've got two at the moment. I'm not afraid of them, and they like me, and yet they do what I tell them.'

'The dogs in the film will be trained.'

She got the part, but she did not realize at the time what a marvellous part it was going to be. However, as soon as she met the director, Charles Crichton, she saw the potential. He was able to breathe humour into the simplest scene. He confided to my mother: 'People seem so surprised. They think I'm too old to be doing what I'm doing. I'm not old – I'm not a hundred yet!'

My mother had no idea what an enormous success the film

would be. She spent only four days filming and never saw any of the other hilariously funny scenes. The only actor with whom she worked was Michael Palin, and she found him delightful, unassuming and modest. Kevin Kline was introduced to her on one of the days, and she met Jamie Lee Curtis – who was having a moustache put on in the make-up room.

It is well known that English people, and in fact many people all over the world, adore their dogs and cannot stand the thought of any cruelty to animals. John Cleese admitted that he was a little concerned about the public's reaction to the three dogs being killed. My mother responded, 'I'm not – I think that people will see the joke. It must be obvious that none of the dogs was really hurt. When the great big Dobermann runs off with one of the dogs, it is only a dummy. In any case, Mrs Cody doesn't deserve to have those dogs – they are better off dead than with her!'

Eventually the film was shown in America, and my mother met John Cleese at a function soon afterwards. 'It is an interesting thing about the dogs,' he told her. 'After the showing in America the audience were coming out, and suddenly I saw this formidable woman coming towards me. I braced myself, preparing for the worst, and she said, "I enjoyed your film immensely, Mr Cleese. There's just one thing wrong with it – you did not kill enough dogs!" '

After the film was finished and edited, John Cleese wrote to my mother thanking her for her performance, and congratulating her on the fact that she was probably the only person who did not have any scenes cut. 'Considering I only had four lines,' she thought, 'it does not mean as much as it appears to mean.'

Early in 1987 an invitation arrived from the Prime Minister and Mr Denis Thatcher requesting the 'Honour' of my mother's company at a Reception for the Arts at 10 Downing Street, Whitehall. She accepted immediately. 'I mistakenly thought that it was from 6.30 onwards instead of 6 p.m. At the beginning of the road there was a barrier, and two policemen standing there. One of them said, "Hallo! Oh, it's you! You're a bit late, aren't you? They've all been here since six o'clock; the press have come and gone."

'I went through the gate, where a few more policemen gave me a big welcome, then up the steps and inside. There were two or three charming women taking coats and giving tickets, who said, "Lovely to see you, Miss Hayes." At the bottom of the stairs a footman gave me a big smile, and directed me to the top of the stairs where another footman pointed to the room in which the reception was being held. I walked across to the footman announcing the guests and gave him my card. He called out, "Miss Patricia Hayes", and I walked forward to where I could see Margaret Thatcher and Denis Thatcher just saying goodbye to previous guests. She turned towards me, took me by the hand and – without looking at me – said "How nice of you to come", passing me swiftly over to Denis. "How very pleased we are to welcome you tonight." "Thank you very much" – neither of them had the faintest idea who I was! I hurriedly left that room and went into another big room which was absolutely full of well-known people. I could see Sir Alec Guinness, Sir John Gielgud, Dilys Powell and Sheila Hancock. I ordered a soft drink, then Sir Alec came over and said, "We didn't meet in *Little Dorrit*!" "No, we didn't." "I have to go now." "I've only just met you. Why have you got to go?" "I have another appointment." So he left, and the next moment Mrs Thatcher walked into the room: "Why don't you spread out? You are all so crowded in this room." Whereupon she ushered me out ahead of her, back into the room where she and Denis had been receiving people. At that moment the footman called, "Sir Roy Strong". Margaret Thatcher said, "Oh, Sir Roy, how are you? I loved your book on the small garden. Unfortunately, we had already made our new garden." Then she turned to me: "He wrote this marvellous book on small gardens, you see." He then said, "And you are standing talking to one of our most famous actresses."

'Whereupon she turned to me, aghast, and said, "Oh, really

– could you tell me your name? We see so little television, and we never get to the Theatre." '

My mother quite understood. And she was nominated for an OBE in the next batch of nominations, a consolation prize, perhaps.